Empowerment of Indian Muslims

About the Editors

Mirza Asmer Beg is Professor of Political Science at the Aligarh Muslim University, Aligarh, India. He is Fellow of Salzburg Global Seminars, Austria. He is the author of *In the Tug-of-War*. He had contributed seven articles to the International Encyclopaedia of Affirmative Action (Greenwood Publishing Company, USA). He has written more than twenty five research papers in national and international journals. He has also contributed more than fifty articles in national dailies.

Abdur Raheem Kidwai is Professor of English and Director of UGC Academic Staff College, Aligarh Muslim University, Aligarh, India. He is also Visiting Fellow at the Department of English, University of Leicester. His publications include *Orientalism in Lord Byron's Turkish Tales*, US/Canada, Lewiston, Mellen University Press, 1995;*The Crescent and the Cross: Image of the Orient in English Literature*, Aligarh Muslim University, 1997; *Stranger than Fiction: Image of Islam/ Muslims in English Fiction*, APH, New Delhi, 2000 (Edited Volume); *Behind the Veil: Representation of Muslim Woman in Indian Writings in English* 1950-2000, APH, New Delhi, 2007 (Edited Volume);*Literary Orientalism: A Companion*, New Delhi, Viva Books, 2009, Higher Education: Issues and Challenges, (Edited Volume), New Delhi, Viva Books, 2010. *The Holy and the Unholy Critical Essays on Qaisra Shahraz's Fiction*. (Edited Volume), New Delhi, Sarup and Sons, 2010.

Empowerment of Indian Muslims

Perspectives, Planning and Road Ahead

Edited by

Professor Mirza Asmer Beg
and
Professor A.R. Kidwai

CONCEPT PUBLISHING COMPANY PVT. LTD.
NEW DELHI-110059

ISBN-13: 978-81-8069-886-6

First Published 2012

Published and Printed by

Concept
Since 1974

Concept Publishing Company Pvt. Ltd.
A/15-16, Commercial Block, Mohan Garden
New Delhi-110059 (India)
T: 25351460, 25351794, *F*: 091-11-25357109
E: publishing@conceptpub.com, W: www.conceptpub.com
Editorial Office: H-13, Bali Nagar, New Delhi-110 015, India.

Cataloging in Publication Data--*Courtesy:* D.K. Agencies (P) Ltd. <docinfo@dkagencies.com>

Empowerment of Indian Muslims : Muslims perspectives, planning and road ahead / edited by Mirza Asmer Beg and A.R. Kidwai.

p. cm.
Includes bibliographical references and index.
ISBN 9788180698866

1. Muslims—Education—India—Congresses. 2. Muslims—Government policy India—Congresses. 3. Muslims—India—Social conditions—Congresses. 4 .Muslims—India—Economic conditions—Congresses. I. Beg, Mirza Asmer. II. Kidwai, Abdur Raheem.

DDC 371.828297 23

Contents

Contributors

Ahmad, Hamida, Formerly Professor, Department of Psychology, A.M.U and Formerly Member, University Grants Commission, New Delhi.

Ahmad, Rais, Associate Professor, Department of Agricultural Economics and Business Management, AMU, Aligarh.
Email: drraisahmad@gmail.com

Alam, Aftab, Associate Professor, Department of Political Science, AMU, Aligarh. Email: aftabalam2004@gmail.com

Beg, Mirza Asmer, Professor, Department of Political Science, AMU, Aligarh. Email: asmerbeg@rediffmail.com

Chauhan, C. P. S., Professor of Education and Dean, Faculty of Social Sciences, Aligarh Muslim University, Aligarh.
Email: cps_chauhan@yahoo.com

Kidwai, Abdul Haleem, Research Associate, Tata Institute of Social Sciences, Mumbai.
Email: ahkidwai@gmail.com

Kidwai, A.R., Director, UGC Academic Staff College, Aligarh Muslim University and Professor of English, AMU, Aligarh.
Email: sulaim_05@yahoo.co.in

Mujaddidi, Mawlana Mohammad Fazlur Rahim, Rector, Jamae-Tul-Hidaya, Jaipur, Rajasthan.

Muzammil, Mohd., Lucknow University, Lucknow.
Email: prof.muzammil@gmail.com

Nehal, Raashid, Associate Professor, Department of English, AMU, Aligarh. Email: nraashid@rediffmail.com

Nomani, Md. Zafar Mahfooz, Associate Professor, Department of Law, Aligarh Muslim University, Aligarh-202002
E-mail: zafarnomani@rediffmail.com

Shabbir, M., (Ambedkar Chair Professor of Law), Dean & Chairman, Faculty of Law and MIC AMU Legal Affairs, AMU, Aligarh.
Email: mshabbir100@ hotmail.com

Talib, Parvaiz, Professor, Department of Business Administration, AMU, Aligarh.
Email: parvaiztalib@gmail.com

Waheed, Abdul, Director, CEPECAMI, AMU, Aligarh and Associate Professor, Department of Sociology, AMU, Aligarh.

Introduction

The present volume has grown out of the papers presented at the Heads of Departments Meet organized as part of UGC Academic Staff College activity. Since social exclusion and marginality studies have their bearing on our educational system, the UGC Academic Staff College, Aligarh Muslim University felt the pressing need for addressing this important and topical issue. It is gratifying that a dozen of AMU faculty members, mostly from the faculty of Social Sciences responded positively to our request for examining in detail the issue of the Empowerment of Minorities in the 12th Plan. The contributors were requested in particular to put forward specific suggestions and recommendations which may help realize the dream of empowering the minorities and of improving their lot. Although these suggestions are directed at the Planning Commission, Ministry of Minorities Affairs and other government agencies, the minorities and NGOs should find this volume of much interest and relevance. It should prompt the minorities to do some soul searching and stock taking in terms of both conceiving and executing remedial actions.

In her paper, Prof. Hameeda Ahmad argues that already existing institutions which are catering to the educational needs of the minorities should be encouraged to grow and develop into quality institutions. Bodies which have the responsibility of addressing the needs or responding to proposals from institutions, particularly institutions catering to Muslim minorities, with special reference to women, should be functional. A high powered Monitoring Committee should oversee the functioning of these bodies. The monitoring committee should include honest and committed stakeholders, educationists and members of the community reputed to have impeccable integrity.

Dr. Rais Ahmad maintains that Muslims may be allowed to set up a huge National Muslim Poor Children's Educational Trust with its branches in all states and states will have its branches in all the districts- urban, semi-urban and in rural areas. This trust will establish schools/polytechnics especially for poor Muslim children who do not go to schools due to poverty and low income of their parents. In addition to this all Waqf Boards in the country will be the active part and parcel of this Trust and it will be having state braches under the control of Waqf Boards. In this programme Waqf Boards can play a very pivotal role by providing for requirement of land for schools, Polytechnics and hostels. Thus this trust specifically meant for poor Muslim children's education will have huge funds for setting up of Schools/polytechnics for poor Muslims in the country.

Dr. Aftab Ahmad argues that Community Target Approach and not Area Target Approach should be adopted - The existing Area Intensive Programme needs to be reviewed and evaluated. There is merit in the argument that conditions of Muslim will not improve by opening more *schools in minority* concentrated districts or blocs but by opening *schools for Muslims.* He argues that at least 15 per cent seats in all non-minority educational institutions should be earmarked by law for the minorities. He adds that the process of transition from Madarsa to modern education should be smooth and simple and for that steps should be taken at national level for the equivalence of Madarsa certificates and degrees to enable the Madarsa products to seek further admissions in the colleges and universities and for their eligibility in competitive examinations. Urdu is of paramount importance for the educational development of Indian Muslims. Facilities for primary education should be provided through Urdu medium to children whose mother tongue is Urdu. In each locality where 10 per cent of the population is Urdu speaking, at least one Urdu medium primary school should be set up. Provision in the 12th Plan must also be made for the establishment of a Minority Residential English Medium School of 12th standard, separately for boys and girls, affiliated to CBSE and on the pattern of Kendriya Vidyalayas in each of the 90 Muslim concentration Districts.

Prof. Mirza Asmer Beg argues that as a matter of state policy, the students who get admission to professional courses should get interest-free bank loans on the sovereign guarantee of the state and economic status of the parents should not matter in these cases. We also need to structure a Waqf Development Corporation, with a dispute redressal forum, at the national level. To empower the Muslims, it is essential to equip them to help themselves. Muslims must be assisted by the Government to set up their educational and financial institutions in a planned manner and for this to be fruitful; we need to set up a National Consultancy Centre For Muslims. Such a Centre would coordinate all welfare activities, where the NGOs, community leaders and the Government would be the main actors. Further we need to have a National Unity Department, which would oversee the efforts towards confidence-building of the minorities. It is also essential to establish a statutory National/State Community Relations Commissions (CRC) for monitoring and resolution of inter-community/group conflicts especially on ethno-religious issues as recommended by the NCM Report 1999.

Prof. CPS Chauhan highlights a shocking fact that at the elementary level enrollment percent of Muslim boys is less than that of Muslim girls. This is a matter of special concern and calls for a deeper probe into the situation. The enrollment figures in higher education in respect of various religious groups are startling in the sense that Muslim community as the largest minority group has the smallest enrollment. While national level GER at higher education stage was more than 12 per cent, it was 19.9 per cent for Christians, 13.1 per cent for Hindus and 12.7 per cent for Sikhs. In the case of Muslims the figure was only 7.7 per cent against their share of 13.4 per cent in the Indian population. In the case of Muslim women the GER was only 6.2 per cent as against 10.9 per cent for Hindu women, 20.0 per cent for Christian women, and 15 per cent for Sikh women.

Prof. A.R. Kidwai suggests that there is an urgent need for the establishment of a *Nodal Agency* for the revitalization for the Muslim Managed Degree Colleges. The creation of such an agency at the

Aligarh Muslim University might help improve the quality of these Colleges. As the Aligarh Muslim University Act of 1920, as amended in 1981 has entrusted the AMU with the responsibility to work for the promotion of the education and cultural advancement of Muslims of India, the UGC Academic Staff College at the AMU is suited best for its role as the *Nodal Agency* for the quality improvement of these Colleges.

Prof. Mohd. Muzammil states that for empowering Muslims in the Plan period, we need to have a national and a sub national Muslim Empowerment Measure (MEM) that needs to concentrate on three points: (i) economic empowerment, (ii) professional empowerment and (iii) political empowerment. Share of Muslims in economic resources can be increased by enabling the Muslim community to have higher per capita income which can be taken as the variable for economic empowerment. Professional empowerment can be accomplished by increasing the access of Muslims to professional opportunities and participation in decision making – enabling them to lead a fuller, richer and more varied life. Professional empowerment can be ensured by enhancing their share in four areas of regular employment (i) professional jobs, (ii) technical jobs, (iii) administrative jobs, and (iv) managerial jobs.

Dr. Rashid Nehal points out that if we look at the data related to allocation of resources for minorities, the per capita plan allocation of resources for minorities in 2010-11 is Rs. 792/- which was even below ST (Rs. 1521/-) and SC (Rs. 1220/). Religious minorities including Muslims constitute 19 per cent of the population whereas budgetary allocations for schemes designed for this section is not more than 5 per cent of total plan allocation. Emphasizing that Madarsas are an increasingly important part of the Indian education System he presents a plan for developing English language teacher training programme aimed at enhancing student performance in Madrasas located in Muslim concentration districts of U.P. and Bihar.

Dr. Zafar Mahfooz Nomani informs that the studies on Muslims in India are generally taken up out of politicization of Hindu-Muslim relationship and channelizing to vote bank politics. This trivializes access, empowerment and equalization of opportunities enshrined in the Constitution. The Right to Equality goes beyond a formal requirement of ensuring absence of direct discrimination and puts a positive obligation on the State to control direct as well as indirect discrimination, eliminate extreme forms of deprivation and take into account the burden of history.

The Muslim studies require a dispassionate reading of contemporary history to locate causes of the process of social exclusion and inclusion leading to the present state of the Muslims and understanding for the appropriateness of corrective measures. The constitution and reports of these committees generally documents the obvious issues in an innovative ways. This also feeds appeasement theory and triggers hostility among a minority of Hindus in the majority community who themselves feel endangered by Muslims. On the other hand, Muslim feels unnecessarily excited about the documented portrayal of their plight and ultimately shocked by perpetual betrayal and deep frustrations. There is need to come out of this doctrinaire legacy and to marshal argument in the vocabulary of equalization of opportunity, guarded by the Constitution, rule of law and democratic governance. The government should not shy away from fair documentation of Muslim condition under census of India in an honest way and search for solutions by equalization. This can be achieved by the proportionate allocation of resources according to population of Muslims and their proper implementation.

Prof. M. Shabbir argues that the word "Minority" must be defined by the Parliament while amending by way of an insertion into Article 29 of the Constitution of India to end conflicting decisions of the judicial branch of the State. He adds that proportionate to the population, the representation of the Muslims in all services under the Union of India must also be ensured by suitably amending the existing law or bringing in a new legislation thereto in the Parliament or otherwise. He further says that Right not to be Poor, Right to be Consulted and Right of Participation in the "Inclusive Economic Growth Model" of Development in every walk of life must also be ensured without any discrimination whatsoever.

Prof. Parvaiz Talib maintains that there is a need to initiate measures to increase the representation of Muslims in elite government jobs. He adds that a substantial section of Muslim population in India is leading life at the periphery. The target group falling in this category comprises those who are *illiterates,* i.e., they have never had access to educational opportunity, *dropouts* i.e. those who did enrol themselves in a school but could not continue their education because of several factors. Then, there is a significant chunk of students who are either studying or have passed out Madarsas - the Islamic Seminaries. There is an urgent need to initiate measures so that this group is able to acquire such skills which helps them earn a reasonable living.

Prof. Talib had an occasion to study and experience a model being initiated and crystallized in southern India. This movement, called the community colleges, is being run under the stewardship of a Jesuit priest Dr. Xavier Alphonse. Launched in 1995 with first Community College, the project has increased manifold, with more than 200 community colleges across India - though majority of them are still located in Tamil Nadu. There is a need for the spread of this model which has been so successfully implemented in Southern India.

Dr. Abdul Waheed opines that all the steps, which the HRD Ministry claimed for educational development of minorities during the 11th plan, were the part and parcel of schemes whose benefits are available either to all citizens of the country or to minorities, SCs, STs, equally. There was nothing exclusively directed at Muslim.

Mr. Abdul Haleem Kidwai argues that micro-level studies are not sufficient to diagnose the underlying ranks of poverty among Muslims. Hence, he stresses upon the importance of micro-level studies. Here he has presented the findings of his study in Govandi, Mumbai, which was further supplemented by fieldwork in Mumbai, Thane.

It is, therefore, suggested that the following proposals may be taken into consideration for the educational empowerment of minorities in 12th Five Year Plan

(a) Unit of administration for such schemes must primarily be locality or habitation, like Ambedkar Village Scheme for SCs, in which 25 per cent and above population is of Muslims. Block or tehsil or district as a unit for administering minority welfare scheme does not ensure the flow of benefits to Muslims.

(b) Multi-sectoral District Development Programme should be transformed into uni-sectoral (Education) development programme and its benefits be extended to all minority concentration habitations.

(c) If any scheme is not implemented during the plan period, unutilized grant either must be carried forward in the next plan or it may be transferred to the corpus fund of Maulana Azad Education Foundation whose grant-in-aid should be available to minorities in the ratio of their population.

(d) A separate budgetary sub-plan must be created for the development of Muslims in the way that governments have done for SCs and STs.

(e) Apart from the creation of Primary and Upper Primary schools as part of the Right to Education Act 2009, co-educational non-residential Senior Secondary Schools of quality education must be created in every rural-urban habitation of Muslim concentration.

(f) Schools, which may be called Learning-Earning schools, may be opened in Muslim artisans concentration localities. These schools would certainly attract children of poor families which, instead of enrolling their children in schools, prefer to send them for either earning or learning some craft.

In the end, we take this opportunity to thank in particular Maulana Fazlur Rahim, Rector, Jamea-Tul-Hidaya, Jaipur, Rajasthan for bringing out the areas in which governmental interventions are deficient and in suggesting operational strategies for future action. Over the years his efforts have been directed towards actualizing affirmative action for alleviating the plight of the Muslim community, especially its educational backwardness. We are grateful also to our colleagues at the Aligarh Muslim University for having contributed their valuable papers. We are thankful to the UGC for enabling us to organize the above programme, which led to bringing out the present volume.

November 2011 **Mirza Asmer Beg**
Aligarh **A.R. Kidwai**

1

Empowerment of Muslims through Quality Education

Hamida Ahmad

It is a universally accepted fact that education is the most potent and effective tool to achieve empowerment of any section of society. Although it is true that economic well-being also makes a significant contribution in this regard, but the nature of positive change brought about by education ensures a position of dignity for the individual and the community which instills a sense of confidence and self-worth. Elevation of social and economic status are usually natural outcomes of good education.

Thus the largest minority of the country which has lagged behind pathetically in the field of education, must set high targets in this sphere. Unless the second largest majority forges ahead and contributes meaningfully to the affairs of this great nation, we will not survive in the competitive global scenario of today. It was with this philosophy that the great visionary Sir Syed Ahmad Khan, established the Aligarh Muslim University. Undoubtedly the movement spearheaded by him contributed greatly in bettering the lot of the Indian Muslims, but this journey upwards received a major setback in the volatile post-partition climate of the country. Problems and challenges became compounded and while other communities went steadily higher up the educational ladder, the Muslim community dived downwards. This is unequivocally brought out by the Sachar Committee report. What Sir Syed prescribed for Muslims more than a century ago still holds good—only good quality, modern education can empower them.

The Sachar Committee was an eye opener because the enormity of the problem was brought out, not in vague, politically populistic terms, but with the support of concrete facts and statistics. The country in general and the Muslim community in particular received a much needed jolt and many well-intentioned programmes have been set in motion. To what extent goods have been delivered needs to be evaluated.

However, expanding the base of the pyramid of education, though undoubtedly important is just one aspect of the problem. Programmes and ventures in this regard have been set in motion for all sections of society with special mention of Muslims at certain points and they need to be continued forcefully. But if we talk of empowerment of a community, it cannot be visualized merely in terms of percentage of persons receiving education of any kind that is available. This would help to project a slightly more optimistic statistical picture than what was observed by the Sachar Committee with regard to educational status of Muslims.

For empowering a community which is represented far below its share in prestigious jobs and bodies which have policy formulation and decision making powers, it is required that access to quality education be ensured for the community. The Sachar Committee brought out the scanty percentage of Muslims in the Administrative and other high profile services and even in sectors where their number is higher, they find a place in the middle or lower rung of the organization. **Therefore, it should be appreciated that the concept of empowerment of the Muslim minorities is linked inextricably to quality of education available to them.** The Twelfth Plan must take cognizance of this and emphasis on promoting quality education must find a place in its pages and in its programme of action. Such programmes have yielded desired results for other sections of the society, regarding whom cognizance had been taken in a serious way and the government had formulated and implemented such programmes. Muslim minorities require a helping hand of this nature to take them forward.

The concept of quality becomes even more important in the present scenario, firstly because in this era of competition, excellence is an essential condition for achievement and empowerment. Secondly, a very major chunk of courses in frontier areas which open up lucrative opportunities are being run as self-financing courses by private institutions and universities, which are beyond the reach of the majority of the Muslim population. Even other than courses in higher education, school education of good quality is getting more and more costly. To reach competitive standards which enable entry into viable courses in higher education, good foundation at school level is essential.

Therefore, steps should be taken to ensure that a sizeable number of Muslims are enrolled in schools of reputed standard. Scholarships which cover tuition, uniforms, books and other incidental costs should be provided. Some remedial education programmes which would help to level gaps arising out of their disadvantageous situation should also be made available. Such inputs will be useful to help students having potential to come up to the same standards as other students and ultimately emerging as students with capacity to participate and excel in higher education in the most viable courses.

To promote quality education amongst Muslims, two types of strategies need to be adopted. The first has been mentioned in the preceding paragraphs namely of ensuring the enrolment of Muslims in prestigious educational institutions both at the school and higher education level. The second is to help already existing institutions catering to the education of the Muslim community to become quality institutions. It is submitted that today even institutions with potential, rather than being encouraged are thwarted in their efforts to expand and develop. This is not a vague, theoretical statement, but is derived from actual experience with an institution having a glorious history, excellent performance in the present and the potential to grow and develop in the future.

The Islamia College Etawah, which functions under the aegis of HMS Educational Association, Etawah, was established in 1889 by Moulvi Basheeruddin, a contemporary of Sir Syed Ahmad Khan. Nationalists like Dr. Zakir Hussain, Maulana Mohd. Ali, Maulana Shaukat Ali, sportsman like Mohd. Shakeel, former captain of

Indian Hockey team and an Olympian, Devesh Singh Chauhan, goalkeeper, Indian Hockey team and an Arjuna awardee, creative artists like Faani Badayuni, Basheer Badr, K. Asif are products of this College. In 1974, the Association took another progressive step. A girls' school was opened by it because the situation of education of Muslim girls in Etawah was dismal. Today the Islamia Girls School and Inter College has risen to the status of one of the best girls' institutions in Etawah. The results in the High School and Intermediate examinations given below, conducted by the U.P. Board vouchsafe that the performance of these students is far superior to the State average.

Year	Pass % (Intermediate)	Pass % (High School)
2004	100.00	100.00
2005	100.00	94.90
2006	100.00	100.00
2007	100.00	100.00
2008	98.82	88.00
2009	98.18	98.92
2010	100.00	98.86

An inter college of this calibre which is catering to the education of girls of the minority community (who may be considered the weaker section of the weakest community) deserves to be encouraged.

However, only the Junior High School has come into grants-in-aid. The High School is still functioning without any financial support. The Intermediate section is also unaided and permission to teach only a few Arts subjects has been given.

The excellent performance of the girls has created aspirations both amongst students as well as parents. Therefore, efforts to obtain permission for offering science stream and computer subjects and other Arts/Social Science subjects have been going on vigorously. All infrastructure requirements have been made available.

But the policy of affirmative action so vociferously advocated by the Sachar Committee appears to exist only as a policy on paper. The apathy and discouraging behaviours so common at every level of the system continue to create hassles and blockages. In this particular case, persistent follow up revealed that at one point of time, the committee responsible to grant permission for teaching of science and any new subject and give recognition to them had not been constituted. Even when such a committee came into existence, permission was not forthcoming because a hefty amount, not mentioned anywhere as a legitimate fee/expense for such recognition was to be given. This may appear to be a paltry matter in today's world in which corruption is the order of the day and scams run into crores. But institutions which are not running self-financing courses where fee can be increased or decreased have no ready pool of money with them for meeting such expenses. It would indeed be a pity if educational institutions are compelled to subscribe to any degree of corruption because ultimately this corruption becomes a vicious cycle which progresses geometrically and erodes good, healthy practices. Educational institutions which are engaged, together with other constructive objectives in the onerous task of character building should not be brought into this fold.

It is, therefore, important that bodies which are responsible for looking into proposals for development and growth and responding to the genuine needs of educational institutions should (a) be functional; and (b) work within a transparent system. Monitoring of such bodies is essential. Stakeholders, educationists and community members of high integrity should be members of a high powered monitoring committee.

Affirmative action should be reflected in giving priority to educational institutions catering to education of Muslim minorities, particularly minority women in matters of grants of financial support and grants-in-aid. There is a long list of institutions waiting to receive such facilities, but arbitrary decisions, mostly to the disadvantage of minority institutions, deprive the Muslim community even further. For a community so backward in education, protective discrimination is justified, even necessary as it fulfils the essential requirement of equity, before expecting that all can perform equally well on a level playfield. Negative discrimination is criminal. Without financial support, the quality of education is bound to go down, for with low salaries, competent and qualified teachers cannot be inducted.

Therefore, a high-powered monitoring committee which ensures justice in terms of financial support for educational institutions run by minorities is important.

Another important issue is the problem of admission of Muslims in schools and colleges recognized as minority institutions. Surveys have revealed that the number of Muslim students studying in Muslim managed schools and colleges is significantly lower than that of their non-Muslim brethren. Procedures for admission vary, but in a large number of recognized minority institutions, the procedure of admission to the school is through a competitive test with cut off point similar for all aspirants. Muslim community which is educationally and socio-economically backward remains behind. As a result, the number of Muslim students is lower than their non-Muslim counterparts, especially at the intermediate level, where cut off point is stricter. These low numbers are also caused by greater number of dropouts amongst Muslims, largely due to pecuniary reasons, but that needs to be addressed by a comprehensive strategy aimed specifically at curbing dropout amongst Muslims. Poor percentage of Muslims in minority institutions can be tackled effectively by lowering the cut off point in the competitive test, thus facilitating their entry. This would undoubtedly be **protective discrimination** and would serve the purpose of promoting justice and equity for a community that is backward. It is expected that a positive push at the entry levels will give opportunity to this group to imbibe the advantages of education, become motivated and rise above its poor and limiting circumstances.

Other problems like delay in recognizing institutions established and managed by Muslims as minority institutions will be effectively addressed by the establishment of a watchdog body, namely the Monitoring Committee which should be constituted with the intention of making it functional, not for fulfilling a recommended requirement merely on paper.

It is submitted that the Twelfth Five Year Plan which is in the process of being prepared must take note of the voice of the Muslim community which desires to march forward, step in step with the best and participate with optimism and enthusiasm in the affairs of the nation.

The following should find a place in the Twelfth Plan:

- While efforts at spread of education to the teeming masses should continue, **attention should also be focused on quality of education.**
- It should be ensured that a sizeable number of Muslims are given admission in prestigious, high quality schools and institutions of higher education.
- Scholarships which cover the high costs of quality education in these institutions should be made available.
- Reservation of certain percentage of seats for Muslim minorities would be the best method to ensure such admissions. This facility should be provided to Muslims.
- Pending a policy on reservation, quality institutions which facilitate the enrolment of Muslim minorities should be given appreciation in the form of incentives.
- Already existing institutions which are catering to the educational needs of the minorities should be encouraged to grow and develop into quality institutions.
- Bodies which have the responsibility of addressing the needs or responding to proposals from institutions, particularly institutions catering to Muslim minorities, with special reference to women, should be functional.
- Working in such bodies should be transparent.
- A high powered Monitoring Committee should oversee the functioning of these bodies. The monitoring committee should include honest and committed stakeholders, educationists and members of the community reputed to have impeccable integrity.
- Protective discrimination should be exercised (a) in giving recognition, e.g., in matters of (minority status recognition

and teaching subjects); and (b) in giving grants-in-aid to institutions catering to education of Muslim minorities.

- Admission policy should facilitate enrolment of Muslim minorities. Wherever there is admission test, the educationally backward Muslim minorities should be admitted at a lower cut-off-point.

With quality education made available and accessible to the Muslim minorities in the Twelfth Plan, it can become truly empowered and with 'minds without fear and heads held high' participate and contribute in carving the destiny of the nation.

2

Empowerment of Minorities in the Twelfth Plan and a National Muslim Poor Children's Educational Trust

Rais Ahmad

So far as minorities in India are concerned Muslims are the largest minority in the country. Majority of this community is educationally and economically extremely backward. Almost all other minorities are educationally and economically better off. According to latest data Muslims are 20-25 per cent in total population of the country. Unfortunately Muslims have not been able to get their due share in total welfare work done by the Government, for economically weaker sections of the society in the country since independence. Different Governments appointed committees from time to time to find out the causes of educational and economic backwardness of Muslims. Amongst these committees the latest one is the Sachar Committee. This committee has clearly revealed that only 4 per cent Muslim population is educated and it is the most educationally and economically backward minority in the country.

We find that the Governments since independence till date at Centre knowingly did not care for having result oriented welfare programmes for Muslims on the pattern of SC/ST. In some parts of the country the position of Muslim community is worse than SC/ST community. Hence, whatever programmes were there for the benefit of Muslims, were implĕmented half heartedly with complicated procedure so that illiterate Muslims could never be benefited from these schemes. Therefore, the educational and economic backwardness of Muslim community could not be improved. Now this situation has emerged as very drastic one. It is the right time that the Government should pay special attention toward Muslim Minority and introduce various welfare schemes in Twelfth Plan for educational and economic improvement of this community on the pattern on SC/ST.

No doubt that our country is a fast developing economy in the world after adopting liberalization policy in 1991 introduced by the then Finance Minister, Hon'ble Mr. Manmohan Singh who is now the Prime Minister of the country. We expect that under the dynamic leadership of Mr. Manmohan Singh and UPA Chairperson Hon'ble Mrs. Sonia Gandhi our country in next one decade will achieve the status of a developed country and top economic power in the world. These dynamic leaders should pay special attention towards this most backward minority of the country and do the needful in true sense to have desired result.

It is irony of the situation that Muslim minority which is 17 per cent of the total population of the country is highly educational and economically backward. It means in the words of Sir Syed Ahmad Khan, "India is beautiful *Dulhan* and Hindus and Muslims are its two beautiful eyes". I will say it in other words that if 20 per cent body of India is in dark, how the world will accept that we are one of the fastest developing countries of the world.

It is observed that since Independence till date, education and economic backwardness of Muslims could not improve and when it is compared with that period it has worsened. Now it is proper time for introducing special welfare programmes for Muslims to improve their educational and economic empowerment as the Government is in the process of planning Twelfth Plan document. The Government should ensure that proper welfare schemes are designed for Muslims on the pattern of SC/ST community and are included in the Twelfth Plan for implementation throughout the country. The SC/ST community is being benefited since independence regularly and even before independence, i.e., 1931. The procedure for getting benefits of Government welfare programmes for Muslims should be as simple as for SC/ST community.

Now time has come that Muslim Community should be given reservation in education/admission in all category of courses including medicine and Employment in all categories of Government Sector jobs including Indian administrative and civil services so as to improve the educational and economic backwardness. Thus Muslim will enter in the mainstream of the country on large scale. More simply it may be said that to control the resentment in Muslims, they should be given reservation in accordance with their shares in total population and the present gap should be reduced by filling the vacant post in all categories specially in army and police on 100 per cent basis of Muslims so as to increase ratio of Muslims in these service sectors at the earliest. This step will help in removing the feeling of frustration in Muslims of ignorance and discrimination and thus the communal harmony may improve in the whole country. The fear of insecurity will disappear from the minds of the Muslim community. Similarly they should be given reservation in Parliament, assembly, municipal corporations, Panchayats and Pradhan, etc., to the tune of 17 per cent or exactly according to their proportion in total population.

Establishment of a National Muslim Poor Chidren's Educational Trust

According to one estimate that there are more than one crore children who belong to BPL families. Here, I would like to mention that 96 per cent of Muslim population fall in the category of low income group as only 4 per cent are educated. Thus the actual figure of Muslim children who are not in a position to go to school due to poverty and illiteracy of their parents may be in multiple of one crore. In addition to the above, Muslims may be allowed to set up a huge National Muslim Poor Children's Educational Trust with its branches in all States, and the States will have its branches in all the districts—urban, semi-urban and in rural areas. This trust will establish schools/polytechnics specially for poor Muslim children who do not go to schools due to poverty and low income of their parents and children are forced to enter into job market to work in different categories/capacities, i.e., in hotels, tea stalls, rickshaw pulling, domestic helper, auto-workshop, beggars, etc.

As a result of these educational and economic factors backwardness in Muslims is continuously increasing sharply. The poverty, illiteracy, inequality in getting opportunities in society are found to be the main cause of giving birth to social evil activities among the human beings throughout the world. In India Muslims are facing the same situation since independence. It is the need of the hour that the remedial measures may be adopted by the Government of India for improving the poor condition of Muslims, otherwise the dream of becoming the most powerful developed country of world may not be achieved on factual basis and the position of 17 per cent minority population of the country will further deteriorate.

The above proposed trust may be set up as an independent autonomous body without involvement of politicians in management and control from top to bottom, i.e., from national level body to village level. In the beginning by allowing the setting of this trust the Government of India may grant some reasonable funds for land and building at Delhi. They may be allowed to accept donation/Zakat funds from people of the country belonging to any religion who belong to any walk of life/companies/associations/NGOs/NRIs and these donations may be exempt from the income tax as in cases of various social working trusts in the country. Similarly donations from other countries, i.e., international agencies/individuals/corporations, etc., will be acceptable to the Trust for the said noble cause. In addition to this all Waqf Boards in the country will be the active part and parcel of this Trust and it will be having State branches under the control of Waqf Boards. Waqf Board will work with the Trust in accordance with the policy of the National Trust. Waqf Board will provide land and funds as much as possible in their concerned State for opening new schools/polytechnics for poor Muslim children and construction of hostels for different schools at different places. In this programme Waqf Boards can play a very pivotal role by providing huge requirement of land for schools, polytechnics and hostels. Thus this trust specifically meant for poor Muslim children's education will have huge funds for setting up of schools/polytechnics for poor Muslims in the country.

These schools will not charge any fee from the children, schools/polytechnics will provide free of cost all books, uniforms, mid-day meals, transportation, boarding in schools/polytechnics all free of cost. Committees will be appointed at national, State, district and village levels to educate the parents in poor Muslim families about the importance of education for their children and motivate them to send their children (both male and female) to schools of the trust where they will have to pay nothing till the students become ready to get employment or self employed according to his/her interest. Thus gradually scenario will be changed. In these school children will get modern education as well as learn Muslim theology and they will become responsible Indian citizens and part of main stream of the country where they get equal opportunities in all walks of life without any discrimination.

These schools will prepare children according to their interest during the period of schooling for different kind of jobs after Matric or any technical course from its maintained Polytechnics and those students who will be found potential for higher studies in the field of science, technology and medicines, will be guided and financial help may also be provided to them for joining any stream of study according to their interest.

Children Dropout at Primary and Secondary Level of Schooling

For such children who left schools at primary and secondary levels of schooling due to poverty and ignorance of their parents, the Trust Schools will provide free coaching to such boys/girls to complete Matric examination under open school system and guide them to do some technical courses in evening programme of the trust's polytechnic. A large percentage of young Muslims fall under this category will enter into the main stream of the country.

Conclusion

In nutshell I can say to that if the above suggestions/recommendations are accepted by the government in its true sense, it will be the beginning of a new era of revolution like that of green revolution, white revolution, blue revolution. This revolutionary step will be helpful in removal of illiteracy among the children belonging to economically weaker sections of Muslim society and eradication of poverty from the country. Similarly, the whole economically weaker sections of the society may be benefited from this kind of setting of Education Trust. In twelfth appropriate reservations to Muslims must be given as suggested in this chapter. Very soon our country will achieve the distant dream of eradication of poverty from the country and achieve the status of most powerful country in the world where people of all religions will have respect for each other's religion and work together, eat together and live together with peace and harmony.

3

Empowerment of Indian Muslims : Education is the Key!

Aftab Alam

Read in the name of thy Lord and Cherisher,
Who Created man, out of a (mere) clot of congealed blood:
Read! And thy Lord is Most Bountiful
He Who taught the use of pen
Taught man that which he knew not

(*Quran, Surah* 96)

Introduction

Muslims in India lag behind in education is a sad commentary on a community whose holy book Quran is derived from the word meaning reading. The very first verse of the Quran "Iqra/bi-ismi rabbika allathee khalaqa...." is an exertion to read. Our Holy Prophet (SAW), said, Seek knowledge from the cradle to the grave. And: Seek knowledge even if it is to be found in a place as distant as China. It is a matter of utter surprise and shock that despite great emphasis of Islam on seeking *Ilm* why its followers in secular India lag behind? The various commissions appointed by the Government of India and independent researchers have repeatedly confirmed the poor plight of Muslim education in India. The situation has become so depressing that if urgent remedial measures are not undertaken the things would slip out of hand. It is matter of common beliefs that unless Muslims educational backwardness is addressed the empowerment of Indian Muslims would remain elusive. The Muslims in India would remain politically marginalized and economically poor unless they overcome their educational backwardness. The education holds the key to the empowerment of Indian Muslims. Education is one of the most powerful factors for the political, social, economic or spiritual development of individuals and communities. It helps individuals to acquire the confidence and capability to match the levels of those who are in the mainstream in society. The founder of this great seat of learning Sir Syed had realized that education was the only remedy for the ills afflicting the Indian Muslims. He regarded modern education as the only means by which the Muslims could be extricated from the quagmire of stagnation and set on the path of progress.

And let me remind you the fact that India cannot march on the path of development and claim to be world leader if majority of its minority community remain educationally backward. If this trend is not arrested it will have the adverse effect pulling down the general growth of the country. It is well stated that if the house of my neighbour is burning my own house cannot remain protected for long period. One day the flame of my neighbour will engulf my house as well. This is simply to lay emphasis on the fact that the task of empowerment of Indian Muslims should be our national concern and priority. This is also not to underplay the fact that it is the Muslim community that has to ultimately alarm the nation about their plight and take initiative so that other can join them in their task of saving the community from complete debacle. There cannot be two opinions on the fact that the government must come out with a comprehensive plan to improve the educational condition of Muslims. But at the same time it is also equally necessary for Muslims to share their own responsibility in coming out of the quagmire and empower themselves educationally. It is only through the joint efforts of State and Muslim community that we can achieve the goal of taking the community out from the darkness of the educational backwardness.

The Eleventh Five Year Plan acknowledged that though previous Five Year Plans have attempted to focus on weaker sections of the society, they have failed to include many groups, especially Muslims, into the development net. Thus it is right time to discuss the concrete proposals that could be presented before the Government for inclusion in the Twelfth Five Year Plan so that we are not missed once again as it happened in the Eleventh Plan. For any proposal for the development of Muslims of India the education must occupy the key position. My presentation is divided into three parts. The first part simply highlights the state of our educational backwardness. The second part deals with attempts made by the Government of India so far to ameliorate the condition. The last and the most important part from the viewpoint of today's meeting, is about future plan of action highlighting what needs to be done.

Educational Backwardness of Muslims

I would begin with looking the problem of Muslims educational backwardness through statistical prism. Though the educational backwardness of Indian Muslims is a known fact but this has of late been quantified and recognized by the Government of India as well. The Government of India for the first time in its New Education Policy of 1986 recognized the Muslims along with neo-Buddhists as educationally backward on national level. Prior to this the Gopal Singh Committee in the 1980s had accounted for the overall marginalization of the Muslims in the country, depicting hardly better off than the *dalits*. The saga of Muslim educational backwardness was once again presented in the Sachar Committee report in 2006. The Sachar Committee findings are a shocking testimony to six decades of institutional neglect and bias that has left the country's Muslims far behind other Socio-Religious Communities (SRCs) in the areas of education, employment, access to credit, access to social and physical infrastructure and political representation. Some of the important and revealing findings of the Sachar Committee in the education fields are as follow:

1. The literacy rate for Muslims (59%) is far below the national average (65%). When compared to the Scheduled Castes and Scheduled Tribes the growth in literacy for Muslims was lower than the former.

2. As many as 25 per cent of Muslim children in the 6-14 years age group have either never attended schools or else dropped out at some stage.
3. Dropout rate among Muslims is the highest at the level of Primary, Middle and Higher Secondary compared to all the SRCs. Only 17 per cent Muslims above the age of 17 years have completed matriculation as compared to 26 per cent for all SRCs.
4. The disparity in Graduate Attainment Rates between Muslims and other categories has been widening since the 1970s in urban and rural areas. The percentage of graduates in poor households pursuing post-graduate studies is significantly lower for Muslims: Hindus General (29 per cent); SCs/STs (28 per cent); OBCs (23 per cent); Muslims (16 per cent).
5. Only one out of 25 undergraduate student's and one out of 50 post-graduate students in 'premier colleges' are Muslims.
6. Muslims are grossly underrepresented in the elite Indian Institutes of Management (IIMs) and the Indian Institutes of Technology (IITs). Enrolment data for the years 2004-5 and 2005-6 show Muslims were only 1.3 per cent of the total number of students in all the IIM courses. In case of the IITs, out of 27,161 students enrolled in all the courses, only 894 (3.3%) were Muslims.
7. The unemployment rate among Muslim graduates is the highest among all Socio-Religious Categories (SRCs), poor as well as non-poor.

After the findings of the Sachar Committee, now the National Sample Survey Organisation (NSSO), a central government body, has reconfirmed that India's largest religious minority is the most backward community in the field of education. The NSSO report titled "Education in India, 2007-08: Participation and Expenditure", says that of 100 Muslims in the education system, just 10 are enrolled in high school and above. Similar ratio for Scheduled Tribes (STs) is 11, Scheduled Castes (SCs) 12 and Other Backward Classes

(OBCs) 14. Muslims' ratio in higher education is lower than even Scheduled Tribes (STs), who are considered most backward. The report also says that high education among urban Muslims is lower than their counterparts in rural areas despite the fact that urban areas have better educational facilities.

Major existing Government Schemes for Muslim Educational Empowerment

Discussion and evaluation on the existing schemes and programmes launched by the Government of India in the educational fields for Muslims is imperative for any future plan of action. It is true that after the deep slumber of several decades, the Government of India has finally awaken and of late recognized, albeit for political reasons, the need to promote education among Muslims who have fallen far behind the national average and even also behind the SCs, STs and OBC in some respects, in the field of education. The Government of India has thus initiated some schemes and programmes, though without bothering about their effective implementation, to ameliorate the situation. Some of the important schemes and programmes are mentioned below. These schemes and programmes were first launched after the submission of the Gopal Singh Committee report under the PM 15-Point Programme issued in 1983 under the premiership of Mrs. Indira Gandhi. Under the 15-Point Programme two main initiatives were taken in the field of education for minorities: (1) organization of coaching classes in minority education institutions to train students from minority communities to compete successfully in the recruitment for various government jobs; (2) and setting up of ITIs and polytechnics in minority concentration areas.

Next forward leap in the direction of educational uplift of Muslims was the National Education Policy 1986 and its Action Programme. Besides mentioning two schemes from the 15-Point Programme, the NPE 1986 also envisaged some other programmes which included both long term and short term measures. Some short term measures suggested include (1) evaluation of textbooks from national integration point of view; and (2) orientation of principals and managers and training of teachers of minority education institutions. The long term measures included (1) setting up of Early Childhood Education Centres in schools and in areas predominantly inhabited by minorities; (2) appointment of linguistic minority teachers and ensure availability of textbooks in minority languages; (3) opening of girls schools, appointment of lady teachers and opening of girls' hostels for minorities; setting up of libraries and reading rooms in minority areas; and (4) laying down of clear guidelines for recognition of minority institutions and timely disposal of applications for recognition.

In 1992, the 1986 Action Programme was revised and certain new measures were envisaged. Some of them include (1) setting up of Women's Community Polytechnics in minority concentration areas; (2) appointment of Urdu teachers in all the Kendriya and Novodaya Vidyalayas located in minority concentration areas; (3) Area Intensive Programme for Educationally Backward Minorities; (4) Modernization of Madarsa Education by introduction of Science, Mathematics and English/Hindi on voluntary basis in Madarsas and Maktabs; (5) encouraging States to establish Madarsa Board to look after minority education; (6) establishment of an Urdu Open University; (7) bringing out Urdu Textbooks; and (8) where situation warrants opening of Urdu medium sections in the existing secondary schools and opening of new Urdu medium secondary/higher secondary schools in Muslim concentration areas.

In 1989, the Maulana Azad Education Foundation (MAEF), was set up to promote education among educationally backward Muslims in general, and Muslim girls in particular. The Foundation has undertaken activities like establishing and expanding schools/ residential schools/colleges/hostels; purchasing laboratory equipments and furnitures; setting up/strengthening vocational/ technical training centre/institutes; providing scholarships to meritorious girls.

In pursuance of the revised Programme of Action (PoA) 1992, two new centrally-sponsored schemes were launched during 1993-94. These are, Scheme of Area Intensive Programme for

Educationally Backward Minorities; and Scheme of Financial Assistance for Modernisation of Madarsa Education. Over a time, it has been felt that all these schemes need to be implemented in an integrated way so as to have wider coverage, greater thrust and visibility of minority education programme. In the Tenth Plan the aforesaid two schemes have been merged to form the Area Intensive and Madarsa Modernisation Programme. The 'Scheme of Modernisation of Madarsa' provides assistance for meeting the salary requirements @ Rs. 3,000 each per month for two teachers in each Madarsa to impart education in non-traditional subjects of Mathematics, Science, English, etc., and one time assistance of Rs. 7,000 to each Madarsa for subject kits and teaching aids as well as another one time assistance of Rs. 7,000 for establishing book banks in each Madarsa.

The erstwhile Area Intensive and Madarsa Modernisation Programme (AIMMP) scheme has been revised as two distinct schemes with effect from November 2008 namely: (i) Scheme for Providing Quality Education in Madarsas (SPQEM); and (ii) Scheme for Infrastructure Development in Minority Institutions/Schools. SPQEM seeks to bring about qualitative improvement in Madarsas to enable Muslim children attain standards of the national education system in formal education subjects. The unique feature of this modified scheme is that it encourages linkage of Madarsas with National Institute for Open Schooling (NIOS), as accredited centres for providing formal education, which will enable children studying in such Madarsas to get certification for class 5, 8, 10 and 12. An outlay of Rs. 325 crore has been provided for the revised scheme of SPQEM for the Eleventh Plan period. During 2008-09, nine States and one UT, i.e., Andhra Pradesh, Assam, Chattisgarh, Orissa, Madhya Pradesh, Maharashtra, Kerala, Tripura, Uttar Pradesh and Chandigarh have been assisted with Rs. 6541.61 lakh as honorarium to 10,214 Madarsa teachers teaching modern subjects in 5,297 Madarsas.

The infrastructure component of the scheme called the Scheme for Infrastructural Development of Private aided/unaided Minority Institutions (IDMI) (elementary and senior secondary schools).

The scheme is focused towards facilitating education of minoriti by augmenting and strengthening school infrastructure in minori institutions including additional classrooms, science/comput laboratories, library rooms, toilets, drinking water facilities, host buildings, etc., in order to expand facilities for formal education children of minority communities. An outlay of Rs. 125 crore the Eleventh Plan was sanctioned. During 2008-09, no grant w given to any minority institution of any State under the schem During 2009-10, grant was given to 22 minority institutions Government of Uttar Pradesh. During 2010-11, till date, grant h been given to 15 institutions of Kerala, 5 institutions of Maharasht and 5 institutions of Madhya Pradesh.

Amelioration of the Condition: What Needs to be Done?

The Central Government has already initiated, as mentioned abov various useful programmes and schemes to improve the educatic condition of Muslims of India. However, no satisfactory record c the implementation of the schemes and programme relating educational uplift of Muslim minorities is available. There are litt empirical studies that have been done to evaluate the existi schemes in terms of ameliorating the condition. Many good schem have failed to see the light of the day due to lackadaisical ar discriminatory approach of the State governments. It is, howev generally believed that if these schemes are implemented wi sincerity and honesty, it will go a long way towards removing Musli educational backwardness. Many of existing schemes ar programmes need serious review and reinforcement. In additic to existing measures the Government of India may also underta the following measures to further boost the ongoing efforts in th direction and to solve the problem of educational backwardness Muslims more expeditiously.

1. **Establishment of National Centre for the Study Muslims of India.**—Non-availability of reliable dat absence of serious analysis, absence of proper institution mechanism for evaluation and monitoring of existi

Muslim related government's schemes and submitting concrete proposals with sensitivity to the needs of the Muslims by the best of talent available on different aspects of Muslim status in India are some of the stumbling blocks in formulating concrete policies for Muslim empowerment. Hence, it is imperative that an autonomous National Centre for the Study of Muslims of India be established under the Twelfth Five Year Plan. The Centre would conduct policy oriented research and surveys on regular and continuing basis on educational, social, political and other aspects of status of Muslims in India. One of the main tasks of this centre would be to develop a data bank to monitor the Muslim participation in education, scholarships, government's schemes on minority education, employment status, etc. The centre would be nodal agency for evaluation and social auditing of the existing schemes relating to Muslim minority. This should work as national resource centre on Muslim Study. This should be a centre of national importance. **(Budget estimate around 15.00 crore.)**

2. A **National Integration and Minority University** with Medical, Engineering, Law and Management faculties in each State having Muslim population exceeding 10 per cent should be established to fulfil the higher education needs of the Muslims and facilitate the Minority Educational Institutions of the region to get affiliation. This step is important in view of the problems faced by the Muslim Minority Higher Educational Institutions in securing affiliation despite constitutional protection accorded to them. This is necessary to ensure Muslims' easy access to Higher education and instil a sense of security in them. To begin with, in the Twelfth Five Year Plan funds for establishment of at least 5 such universities one each in the State of **West Bengal, Assam, Bihar, Maharashtra** and **Kerala** must be provided.

   All unnecessary impediments must be removed from the procedure and process of recognition of an institution as a minority one. Procedure for establishment and recognition of minority institutions should be liberalised and unnecessary hurdles should not be created in the way of community efforts to create their institutions. It has been reported time and again that authorities concerned refuse to recognize minority institutions on flimsy technical grounds or use delaying tactics to postpone recognition inordinately. **(Budget estimate for each university would be around 500 crore leading to total cost of 2,500 crore.).**

3. **Community Target Approach and Not Area Target Approach should be adopted.**—The existing Area Intensive Programme needs to be reviewed and evaluated. There is merit in the argument that Muslim condition will not improve by opening more *schools* ***in minority*** concentrated districts or blocks but by opening ***schools for Muslims*** or reserving certain percentage of seats for them in the educational institutions opened in these areas. The reasons are very obvious. In the absence of such reservation it is most likely that the benefits of these programmes would not reach to the Muslims as the dominant majority community will easily usurp them. It is thus logical to demand for reservation in admissions. The Rangnath Mishra Committee has already worked out formula in this regard. The Committee argues that as by the force of judicial decisions the minority intake in minority educational institutions has, in the interest of national integration, been restricted to about 50 per cent, thus virtually earmarking the remaining 50 per cent or so for the majority community—we strongly recommend that, by the same analogy and for the same purpose, at least 15 per cent seats in all non-minority educational institutions should be earmarked by law for the minorities. A suitable legislation need to be brought out to give effect to this measure. In the first phase a modest attempt may be made by introducing the quota for Muslims in at least all the Central Universities, IITs and IIMs.

4. **Madarsa Modernization.**—The Madarsa education occupies pre-eminent position in the education delivery system to Muslims in India. The Madarsa Modernization programme should be renamed as **Madarsa Development Programme** as the word "Modernization" is conveying a negative image of Madarsas and giving birth many apprehensions in the minds of Muslims about the true intention of the Government. There are many people who even question the desirability/possibility of any modernization of Madarsas.
   - There is urgent need to convince those who are running Madarsas that their fear are misplaced and modernization does not mean compromising faith and the whole programme of modernization can take place within the framework of Islam.
   - Job-oriented education and vocational training should be introduced in these Madarsas to enable Muslims coming from lower middle classes consisting of artisans, etc., to find education in Madarsa even more relevant. For that special grants should be provided under the Madarsa Development Programme.
   - The process of establishing **Central Madarsa Board** should be accelerated to coordinate and regulate Madarsa education in the country. In the beginning it should be on voluntary basis simply to allay the fear among the some sections of the Muslims that the Government wants to take over the entire Madarsa system. In any attempt to modernize Madarsa education taking into confidence of the community is very important.
   - The process of transition from Madarsa to modern education should be smooth and simple and for that steps should be taken at national level for the equivalence of Madarsa certificates and degrees to enable the Madarsa products to seek further admissions in the colleges and universities and for their eligibility

in competitive examinations. This will also help them in seeking employment in government, semi-government, private and multinational sectors.

- The benefit of existing scheme of providing teachers for English, Social Studies, Mathematics and Science in Madarsas should be extended to all Madarsas.
- A separate Madarsa Teachers Training Institute should be established in each State to provide in-service training to them.
- The disparities in the salaries of science teachers in other schools and Madarsa teachers, who are usually paid very low salaries, should be removed.
- Production of suitable science resource material in Urdu for use in Madarsas and its distribution is prerequisite for introducing and sustaining science education in Madarsas. The task of designing science curricula and production of textbooks for Madarsas could be handed over to the NCERT.

5. **Promotion of Urdu and Opening of Urdu Medium Schools.**—Urdu is of paramount importance for the educational development of Indian Muslims. There are at least five States where more than 10 per cent of the total population claims Urdu as their mother tongue. The virtual exile of Urdu from the schools in several States, both as a medium of instruction and a subject of study is one of the vital factor that have kept the Muslims from utilizing the existing educational facilities provided by the Government in public schools. The Kendriya Vidyalayas located in non-Hindi speaking States have no provision for teaching of Urdu as one of the languages under the three language formula, not even as a third language. Even in Hindi speaking States most of these Vidyalayas are required to teach either one of the South Indian languages. There are very few schools that have provision of teaching of one or the other modern Indian languages that also include Urdu and out of this small number there are very few that opt

for Urdu teaching. In Uttar Pradesh which has the largest Urdu speaking population in India (about 29%), the position of Urdu is most depressing. Furthermore in States where Urdu medium is allowed there is general complaint of non-availability or delay in supply of school textbooks in Urdu and this seriously hampers the progress of Muslim students opting for Urdu medium. It has also been reported that this has sometimes compelled these students to either change the medium of education or leave the education itself. In the light of importance of the Urdu for the educational upliftment of Muslims following measures are needed to be adopted in addition to existing ones:

- Facilities for primary education should be provided through Urdu medium to children whose mother tongue is Urdu. In each locality where lives 10 per cent Urdu speaking population, at least one **Urdu medium primary school** should be set up. In areas where Urdu speaking population is less than 10 per cent, there should be provision for a Urdu teacher. There should be also provision of one Urdu medium **higher secondary** school for every eight to ten Urdu medium primary schools, and also provision of **secondary schools** wherever the Urdu speaking population of an area constitutes 10 per cent of the total population, as suggested by the Committee for the Promotion of Urdu way back in 1975. Implementation of these measures would attract more Muslim students to modern education.
- Under the Twelfth Plan the Government of India should provide funds for establishing 338 Urdu Medium Schools in towns/cities having a substantial minority population as identified by the Government.
- There should be adequate provision for the **training of Urdu teachers** as it is one of the serious problems faced by the Urdu medium schools. Three Academies for Professional Development of Urdu Medium

teachers at JMI, AMU and MANU have been established. There is need to evaluate the performance of these academies.

- Establishment of one **National Urdu University** in each State on the pattern of MANU where Urdu speaking population exceeds 10 per cent.
- Ensuring the **timely availability of textbooks in Urdu** by simultaneous translation and providing incentives to booksellers who keep Urdu books for sale.

6. **Minority Career Counselling, Employment and Placement Cell** in each Muslim concentrated District should also be established under the Twelfth Plan to facilitate and guide educated Muslim youths in selecting right career and to ensure placement for them through their concerted efforts. As it has been found that a large number of educated Muslims wander in search of suitable employment despite attaining required qualifications.
7. **Remedial and Supportive Coaching and Coaching for Competitive Examinations.**—It is generally observed that educationally backward sections of the people, particularly first generation learners usually lag behind in their classes and it also results into more and more dropout. They are required to be provided with supportive coaching which may be arranged in the schools itself. Various coaching schemes of the Government of India do exist today, what is needed now is to implement them effectively and manage them efficiently.
8. Provision in the Twelfth Plan must also be made for the establishment of a **Minority Residential English Medium School** of twelfth standard, separately for boys and girls, affiliated to CBSE and on the pattern of Kendriya Vidyalaya in each 90 Muslim concentrated District. The need of feeder institutions for Muslim higher educational institutions has long been felt. One of the reasons why we are not getting good Muslim students for our higher institutions is the absence of good quality Senior Secondary

Schools in the Muslim locality. The Sachar Committee rightly observed that the Muslims are at a double disadvantage with low levels of education with low quality education. The higher educational institutions would be of no use to Muslims if we are not producing good students for such institutions and the benefits would be availed by other advantageous sections of the society.

9. **Hostel Facility.**—One of the main difficulties faced by Muslim students in the cities is finding suitable accommodation at affordable price. In view of this Muslim Hostels should be built in Muslim concentrated districts. There should be provision for separate hostel facilities for Muslim girls.
10. **Muslim Women Education.**—The state of education among Muslim women is even the worst. The cultural traditions do not allow Muslim girls to take advantage of co-educational schools, especially if they are far away from their homes. The opening of separate girl schools, appointment of lady teachers, and opening of girls hostel are some important measures if implemented sincerely may give boost to Muslim female education. This would facilitate higher participation of girls in school education. To attract more Muslim girls to education special scholarship schemes for them should be introduced.
11. **Secularization of State Education.**—One of the factors that keep Muslims away from government or government aided schools is the cultural environment of the schools. Most of the textbooks for Hindi, History and social sciences are full with Hindu mythology, biased version of Indian history, and misrepresentation of Islam. These textbooks contain some materials which militate against their religious beliefs and way of life. All that make Muslims hesitant of sending their children to schools and in some cases even lead to their withdrawal from schools as well. It is against this background urgent steps must be undertaken to secularize the State education system to instil confidence among Muslims.

12. **National Overseas Scholarships.**—National Overseas Scholarship Scheme for Muslim minority should also be formulated similar to those for SCs and STs so that OBC students can also go abroad for better educational and professional courses which are generally not available in the country.

4

Muslims in India : An Action Plan

Mirza Asmer Beg

Minority rights are enshrined in the Constitution of India. In principle, India is a secular country based on the concept of equality and rule of law. We are signatories to the ICCPR and India was also a party to the UN Declaration on Minorities in 1992. However, at the operational level, the discourse on minorities in India gets defined and limited by the communalism *vs.* secularism framework. It now needs to be placed in the context of the national mainstream efforts, which are directed at ensuring equal rights for all Indians. Of all the religious minorities in India, it is Muslims alone whose existential conditions demand for urgent remedial measures. Their backwardness has been documented by several Government Commissions and reports, which have proved beyond doubt that Muslims lag behind other communities, in all fields.

Muslims in India are faced with many problems. They find themselves in a tight corner with very little room for manoeuvrability. But a basic failure of the community in general has been their inability to define their problems in concrete terms and to think of effective methodologies to tackle these problems. In view of the failure of the Muslims to define their problems and to shape their agenda, this has been done by 'others'. Usually it has been the Government which has performed this task. Their agenda has been set by the successive Governments, ably assisted by the media and other forces inimical to them, and Muslims have only responded to this thoughtlessly. Not only were the problems of Muslims defined by the Government, but it also prescribed remedies. Whether the definition was proper or not, or the prescriptions were useful or not, the Government was least concerned. The Muslim community never tried to intervene in this discourse. It never acted on its own, it only reacted to what was presented before it as 'the problem'. Although, Muslims were the rightful stakeholders in this exercise, but no effort was made to involve them in this process, nor did they make any concerted effort to enter into this process. In view of the all too evident apathy and insensitivity of Government, their real problems have never figured on the agenda, and they have only been responding to pseudo-issues, which have time and again been thrust on them as their agenda. Hence, it has been the issue of maintenance of divorced Muslim women for several years later it was the issue of Babri Masjid, interspersed with a frequent dose of communal riots, which have never let the Muslims think seriously about their real issues, and the operational strategies to tackle them.

In the present times, there is no dearth of evidence in the public sphere, of the all too evident backwardness of the Muslims of India. The Government too, after long years of dilly-dallying, has apparently come to the general understanding that something needs to be done as regards the existential problems of Muslims, who constitute about 14 per cent of the Indian population and but for their uplift, one cannot think of the development of the country. The Government's intent has also been outlined by the Prime Minister recently, when he emphasized upon 'inclusive-growth', while presiding the full meeting of the Planning Commission on the 21st of April, 2011.

However, a basic reason why a number of well-advertised Government initiatives have not yielded the desired results, has been the abysmally low budgetary allocation for programmes directed at socio-economic development of this historically disadvantaged community. The per capita Plan allocation for minorities in 2010-11 was as low as Rs. 797, below even allocations for Scheduled Tribes, which was Rs. 1,521, and for Scheduled Castes, who got Rs. 1,228. Religious minorities, including Muslims, constitute about 19 per cent of the population of India, but budgetary allocations for schemes designed for them is a little over five per cent of the total plan allocations.

Against this backdrop, it seems important that Muslim intellectuals should take the lead in articulating the rightful grievances of the community, and communicating them to the Government in the form of implementable proposals. And more importantly, then following them up, to see the extent to which they actually benefit the community. Monitoring the implementation of Government initiatives for Muslims is important, because we have seen in the past that most schemes earmarked for minorities in India, have remained only on paper, and the real beneficiaries have been almost insignificant.

All these years, whenever the Government has implemented programmes to uplift the depressed sections of the Indian society, it has conveniently left the Muslims out of it. In 1950, when the Government initiated an affirmative action plan to uplift *dalits*, it excluded Muslim *dalits*. In 1989, when the Government initiated the Mandal Commission affirmative action plan for the OBCs, it again left out the Muslim OBCs. With about half of the Indian Muslims belonging to either SC or OBC category, such exclusion from affirmative action plans has caused further deterioration in the educational and socio-economic status of the Muslim community.

The Way Ahead: In view of the precarious condition of the Muslims of India, we suggest certain initiatives, which if woven in the policy framework, may in the long run, benefit the community.

1. An important area of concern is financial support for those Muslim students who intend to go for higher studies. The process of getting educational loans for students in general and Muslim students in particular is very difficult. It will be interesting to study what per cent of such loans have gone to Muslim students. One reason is the fact that Muslims are not able to provide collateral security to the banks for such loans. The banks appear to be reluctant to provide loans to Muslim students without a foolproof

security, in spite of the Government guidelines. The result is that even those Muslim students who qualify for admission to professional courses are not able to get loan from the banks and are forced to dropout. *As a matter of state policy, the students who get admission to professional courses should get interest-free bank loans on the sovereign guarantee of the state and economic status of the parents should not matter in these cases. This will not cost much, but will remove a great impediment in the way of poor Muslim students. The procedure for securing loans should be the same as applicable in case of SC students, and the onus in case of non-utilization of these loans should be on the disbursing body.*

2. The issue of poverty of Muslims of India can be addressed in a big way by one single action, i.e., the development of Wakf properties. India has around four lakh acres of wakf land, half of which has been encroached upon or is under dispute. Even if the remaining half is properly developed, there would be no dearth of finances for welfare of Muslims. *The Ministry of Minority Affairs needs to take up this issue and prepare a plan for Wakf development. An institutional structure needs to be put in place to develop Wakf properties. We already have a Joint Parliamentary Committee Report on Wakf, but no subsequent Action taken Report has been presented, which shows the callousness and apathy as regards this serious issue. The JPC Report says that if Rs. 10,000 crore are invested for developing the Wakf properties, the Muslim community can have an yearly income of Rs. 10,000 crore. Hence, we need to structure a Wakf Development Corporation, with a dispute redressal forum, at the national level.*
3. A lot of initiatives for uplift of Muslims have always been taken by well-meaning individuals as well as groups of people or NGOs, but in the face of the complexity and enormity of problems, their efforts quite often lose focus, and they get disillusioned after some time. In many instances there is duplication, as the initiatives are not coordinated. Many of these initiatives manage to get

support from the state, but as there is no central coordination, the impact of these efforts does not reach the desired level. *To empower the Muslims, it is essential to equip them, to help themselves. Muslims must be assisted by the Government to set up their educational and financial institutions in planned manner and for this to be fruitful we need to set up a National Consultancy Centre for Muslims. Such a Centre would coordinate all welfare activities, where the NGOs, community leaders and the Government would be the main actors.*

4. An important area of concern for Muslims has been the issue of security. Muslims have all these years reconciled to living as second class citizens, provided their security is ensured. Thousands of communal riots since independence have created such a fear psychosis among Muslims that they have not only shrunk in their physical ghettoes, in cities and towns, but their thinking has also been affected by this existential condition. The concern for security has been uppermost in their minds, and once it is taken care of, they are satisfied and do not care to demand their rightful share in the national cake. Many a government has taken advantage of this fear in the 'Muslim Mind', by not doing anything for them, except for giving them physical security, and getting their votes. Bihar under Laloo Yadav, U.P. under Mulayam Singh Yadav and West Bengal under the Left Front are glaring examples. Hence, Muslims have actually been viewed by political parties only as vote banks, whose votes can be garnered by playing with the ever lurking fear of security in their minds. The basic reason for this fear is the conduct of police and para-military forces in situations of communal conflict. Several commissions of enquiry set up by the Government have clearly indicted the local administration and police force for partiality and high-handedness. The Sixth Report of the National Police Commission stated that "one main reason for the lack of objectivity on the part of the police force is the composition

of the police force itself, which is heavily over-weighed in favour of the majority community". *To instil confidence among the Muslims and to give them a sense of security, we suggest that a Multi-religious Police Force Academy be set up, which would be entrusted with the task of recruiting and training police personnel for multi-religious policing. The composition of this police force would resemble the diverse nature of the society. In a communally charged situation, the policeman should perceive of the community, which he is policing, as an ally and not as an enemy. What creates the biggest fear among the minority community, in such a situation, is a biased police force. We suggest that in a situation like this, the multi-religious police force, (like they have in Switzerland and Macedonia) which polices a Muslim majority area, should have a majority of Muslims. A multi-religious police force was also suggested by the Sorabjee Model Police Drafting Committee (2006). Their exercise of authority should be regulated by defined procedures, and any misuse should be subject to the severest punishment. Nothing can generate more confidence and dispel the fear among Muslims, than the understanding that the police force which has been deployed for their security would at least try to come true to its mandate and it does not view them as enemies. We need to have quotas in the police force for different religious groups on the lines of Lebanon, Cyprus and Belgium. We also need to have a National Unity Department, which would oversee the efforts towards confidence-building of the minorities. It is also essential to establish a statutory National/State Community Relations Commissions (CRC) for monitoring and resolution of inter-community/group conflicts especially on ethno-religious issues as recommended by the NCM Report 1999.*

5. The country needs authentic, empirical and high quality research on Muslims and their problems. This would form the basis of policies directed towards them. There is a big lacuna in this regard in India. No workable policy can be structured in the absence of such data. This gap needs to

be bridged, more so, because the Twelfth Plan has recognized Muslims as a separate category, Earlier they were grouped under the blanket category of 'minorities'. *We propose that a high quality Research Centre be set up by the Government of India, which should be tasked with doing research on issues concerning Muslims. It should build an authentic national data-base on Muslims.*

6. Of all the minority welfare schemes which the Government of India has launched, we need to see that their benefits are maximized by the minorities. For this we need *legally binding implementation mechanisms. The Government needs to be made accountable for shortfalls.*
7. Muslims are educationally backward and, therefore, there share in skilled employment is very low. However, some sections among Muslims complain that their share in Government jobs is low because of the discriminatory attitude of the recruiting bodies. Although it is difficult to empirically substantiate these charges, but if we look at the representation of Muslims in category C and D jobs, where educational qualifications are minimal or non-existent, one is forced to consider the discrimination thesis seriously. *We propose that in keeping with the Twelfth Plan's emphasis on inclusive growth, provisions should be made for better representation of Muslims in jobs where their educational backwardness is not a handicap for them. The departments which give better representation to Muslims must be given incentives for opting for diversity, and those who do not go for it, must be penalized. Diversity should also be promoted in the private sector and in habitats as well. Those employers, who do not comply, should be asked to explain in writing, the reasons for non-compliance on this count.*
8. Any initiative of the Government directed towards the uplift of the Muslims of India, is often construed by a section here as another instance of appeasement of Muslims. Such a pernicious viewpoint gets more acceptability when the educational system lends credence to such falsehoods and

half-truths by propagating them through textbooks. School books are full of canards and stereotypes and caricatures of Muslims. *It is, therefore, essential to set up an independent National Commission on Education to see that education does not become an instrument of propagating myths and exclusivism. We need an education system which is multi-culturally oriented.*

9. A favourite stick of the communalists which they use against Muslims is the Hajj subsidy. It is an interesting case of the Government fleecing the poor Muslims and then parading it as an instance of favouring Muslims. Moreover, the Government, despite repeated objections to this, maintains that it would not shirk from its responsibility of helping the Hajis. Actually, the Air India charges Rs. 85,000, per person as return fare to Saudi Arabia. The usual fare with any other carrier would be not more than Rs. 35,000, if one does not go through the Hajj committee. So going through the Government channel is more expensive than through a private agent, for whom it is a profit-making venture. But then the Government says, it is a chartered flight. However, when all seats in this chartered flight are booked, the cost-benefit balance of running this flight should be the same as any other flight. But the Government charges more than double the actual cost and then presents it as a favour to Muslims going to Hajj. *It is high time now that the Hajj subsidy is stopped and a National Corporation be set up to oversee the Hajj programme for Indian Muslims. All other such pseudo provisions must be withdrawn instantly as they do not yield any benefits to the community, but give ammunition to Muslim-bashers to further corner the community. The Hajj subsidy is a classic case of stigmatization of Muslims in the public sphere in spite of actual discrimination, masquerading as favour.*

10. For India to develop peacefully, it is essential that all citizens get equitable justice from the system. *The first step towards secular justice, which is the bare minimum requirement of any secular state, would be for the Government to publish—1. all*

informations about ex-gratia compensation/relief paid to all sufferers of disturbances at least since 1980-81; 2. all informations on riot related cases filed, investigation/prosecution and conviction or cases dismissed/withdrawn with reasons of dismissal and withdrawal since 1980-81; 3. all informations on targeted killings/encounter killings of Muslims and custodial crimes against them with hate motive; 4. all informations on detainees under counter-terror operations. This is important to counter all kinds of canards and distortions which shape our perception and thinking.

The above-mentioned suggestions are intended as inputs to the policy-making bodies of the Government of India. As the problems are complex and deep-rooted, we do not intend to give some quick and easy solutions. It is going to be a long term national enterprise. We have to build bridges of goodwill and understanding across India. We need to appreciate and make every Indian understand that the problems of Muslims in India are not the problems of this community alone, they are problems of the Indian nation, and they have to be tackled as challenges to all of us. It is the Government's basic responsibility to assist the destitute Muslim community out of poverty and exclusion.

5

Participation of Indian Muslims in Educative Process

C.P.S. Chauhan

Traditionally, the Indian society was divided into four major occupational classes, known as *varnas* (meaning colours)—*Brahmins, Kshatriyas, Vaishyas, and Shudras*. Historically, this classification was based on the principle of division of labour. *Brahmins* (teachers, scholars and priests) constituted the educated and respectable class which was at the top of the hierarchy. *Kshatriyas* (kings and warriors) had the responsibility of protecting the society and state from external threats. *Vaishyas* (producers and protectors of wealth), who ranked third, would take care of the economy and supply of food. *Shudras* (service providers), the lowest in the hierarchy, had the responsibility of serving the upper three classes (Ghurye, 1969). There is lack of consensus among sociologists on the relation between *varna* and caste. Some argue that *varna*, which has its origin in the ancient Indian literature, is the source of the concept of caste. The Indian sociologists have tried to perceive the phenomenon of caste in terms of *varna* (Srinivas, 1962) indicating that each *varna* embodied people professing different occupations, more or less of the same level, which formed sub-classes known as castes or *jatis*. Each *jati* was a hereditary and endogamous group, generally with occupation-based nomenclature. Thus, there were thousands of castes having their origin in the four major *varnas*, all asserting their separate identities, and consequently, increasing the number of castes.

Over the centuries, the structure of Indian society has

undergone considerable change with the arrival of people from different parts of the world for various purposes and settling here. Now, India is a multi-religious society with people professing different religions living together. Though, a large majority of the people professes Hinduism, there are people in significant numbers, who profess other religions also. About 20 per cent of the people have faith in other religions such as Islam, Christianity, Sikhism, Buddhism, Jainism and others. These religious groups are termed as 'minorities' each being smaller in number as compared to the Hindu majority. The term 'minority' has not been properly defined in the Constitution of India. The Constitution also does not lay down objective criteria for labelling a group as minority. The U.N. Sub-Commission on Prevention of Discrimination and Protection of Minorities has defined minority as follows:

(1) The term 'minority' includes only those non-documents groups of the population which possess and wish to preserve stable ethnic, religious or linguistic traditions or characteristics markedly different from those of the rest of the population;
(2) Such minorities should properly include the number of persons sufficient by themselves to preserve such traditions or characteristics; and
(3) Such minorities should be loyal to the state of which they are nationals.

In India, the term minority is usually used to denote any religious community whose members tend to assert their distinctiveness in relation to the Hindu majority. Accordingly, Muslims, Christians, Sikhs, Buddhists, Jains, Parsis and Jews are commonly labelled as minorities. While people are free to profess and preach their own faith, there are common cultural threads which maintain social coherence and keep the society united. After independence, India has made tremendous progress in all fields the credit of which goes to its strong education system. While overall educational development of the society has taken place, some social groups including minorities have remained educationally backward.

Among the minorities, Christians, Sikhs and some other small religious groups have kept pace with the rest of the society in educational development taking full advantage of the constitutional provisions meant for this purpose. Generally, the question of educational backwardness is raised only in the case of Muslims. In this chapter, the author has focused his attention on the issues related to educational status of Indian Muslims minority and their implications for policy formulation.

Demographic Profile

Indian society is known for its secular outlook with people of different religions living together. While Pakistan became a theocratic state (Islamic Republic of Pakistan) after partition of united India in 1947, the independent India chose to remain a democratic country with socialistic and secular values enshrined in the Constitution. Over the years minorities have become inseparable constituents of our population. There has been considerable change in the size of their population since the Census of 1951 (Table 5.1). While per cent share of Hindu majority in the total population has gone down from 85 in 1951 to 80.5 in 2001, the share of minorities has gone up proportionately. It is likely that 2011 Census Report will present a new picture.

Table 5.1: Indian Population by Religion (*per cent*)*

Groups	*1951*	*1961*	*1971*	*1981*	*1991*	*2001*
Hindu	85.00	83.50	82.70	82.60	82.40	80.50
Muslim	9.90	10.70	11.20	11.40	11.70	13.40
Christian	2.30	2.40	2.60	2.40	2.30	2.30
Sikh	0.70	1.80	1.90	2.00	2.00	2.00
Buddhist	–	0.70	0.70	0.70	0.80	0.80
Jain	–	0.50	0.50	0.50	0.40	0.40
Others	1.10	0.40	0.40	0.40	0.40	0.60
Total	100.00	100.00	100.00	100.00	100.00	100.00

*Compiled from different sources.

According to the 2001 Census, minorities constitute about 19.5 per cent of the people of India. Out of total population of 1,028 million, 827 million (80.5%) were Hindus, 138 million (13.4%) Muslims, 24 million (2.3%) Christians, 19 million (2.0%) Sikhs, 7.9 million (0.8%) Buddhists, 4.2 million (0.4%) Jains and 6.6 million (0.6%) were others. Let us have a glance over the demographic profile of various religious groups in terms of the trend of their population growth. This will give us some idea about the magnitude of the problem of educational backwardness which is the main focus of this chapter. Along with the overall population of India, the population of minorities has also increased over the last six decades since independence. As mentioned earlier, all minorities except *Muslims* have kept pace with the overall educational development in the country. Christians, Sikhs, Jews, Parsis and Jains have taken care of their own education and are, in fact, more advanced educationally than the total population. It is only the *Muslim* community that has been an educationally backward religious minority and a subject of concern for the Government of India. Muslims constitute the largest religious minority in the country—about 13.4 per cent of the total population. It may be observed that among all minorities the growth rate of Muslim population has been the highest—even greater than national average national population growth rate. Explanation lies in the lack of requisite education and resulting poverty.

It has been rightly stated by a Muslim scholar (Shah, 1983) that there has been a continuous degeneration of Muslims during the post-independence period, which has manifested itself in various forms, such as, poor performance of Muslim candidates in Civil Services Examinations, lack of adequate appearance in the merit lists of High School, Higher Secondary and College Examinations, and sometimes, in the form of inferiority complex as exhibited in the state of indifference towards pressing for their rights and privileges. The poor, economically backward and least educated Indian Muslims cannot join the national main stream unless they advance educationally in all fields, especially, in science and technology. If 13.4 per cent of the people of India remain under-developed and incapable of participating effectively in the developmental processes, its economy will remain handicapped and crippled in the same proportion. These considerations led the framers of the Constitution to introduce specific clauses intended to ensure educational, social, economic and cultural advancement of minorities in free India.

Constitutional Safeguards

The Constitution of India has guaranteed certain privileges to minorities through Articles 28, 29 and 30 in order to ensure their cultural, social and educational well-being. As mentioned in the Preamble of the Constitution, India is a secular country and, therefore, does not provide any kind of official support to any religion. However, the Constitution provides each citizen of the country a freedom to practice any religion of his choice. In view of this, the Constitution makes special provisions related to the status of religious instruction in the institutions funded by the state. The Constitution also provides special safeguards for the educational and cultural interests of minorities. The constitutional status of religious instruction in educational institutions is described in Article 28, which states:

(i) No religious instruction will be provided in any educational institution wholly maintained by the state funds.

(ii) Nothing in clause (i) shall apply to any educational institution, which is administered by the state, but has been established under any endowment or trust, which requires that religious instructions shall be imparted in such institution.

(iii) No person, attending any educational institution recognized by the state or receiving aid out of state funds, shall be required to take part in any religious instruction, that may be imparted in such institution or any premises attached thereto, unless such person or, if such person is a minor, his guardian has given his assent thereto.

As evident from the statements of various clauses of Article 28, religious education is permitted in the institutions established by minorities under any trust or endowment, but nobody can be forced to receive such instruction against his will.

The cultural interests of minorities are protected through Article 29, which states:

(i) Any section of citizens residing in the territory of India or any part thereof having a distinct language, script, or culture of its own shall have the right to conserve the same.
(ii) No citizen shall be denied admission into any educational institution maintained by the state or receiving aid out of state funds on grounds only of religion, race, caste, language or any of them.

All minorities are allowed to conserve their distinct language, script or culture under the above clauses of Article 29, but admission to any educational institution cannot be denied to any citizen on the ground of religion, caste, race or language. This means that doors of all educational institutions are open to every citizen of India irrespective of his religious affiliation.

The educational interests of minorities are protected through Article 30, which states:

(i) All minorities, whether based on religion or language, shall have the right to establish and administer educational institutions of their choice.
(ii) The state shall not, in granting aid to educational institutions, discriminate against any educational institution on the ground that it is under the management of a minority, whether based on religion or language.

Article 30 is the most significant for minorities under which they can establish and run educational institutions of their own choice and the government would treat such institutions at par with other public institutions for the purpose of granting aid from state funds. Since 1947, minority communities have been establishing and administering their own educational institutions at all levels from elementary schooling to university education.

Specifically, Christians have created a huge system of schools and colleges which not only cater to the needs of their own community but also have earned a reputation of providing quality education to the children of other communities.

Avenues of Education for Muslims

There are two major avenues open for education of Indian minorities including Muslims:

(i) National mainstream system of school and college education, and
(ii) A large network of educational institutions (called Madarsas) established under Article 30 of the Constitution.

Despite these provisions and facilities, Muslim community is rated as the most educationally backward minority in India. It appears that this section has not been able to utilize the constitutional provision to their fullest advantage. However, they have created a system of religious education popularly referred to as 'Madarsa Education'. Madarsa is a term used to denote a traditional Arabic or Urdu medium of educational institution set up and managed by Muslim individuals and/or religious bodies. As a conservative estimate, the total number of Madarsas is nearly 35,000 mainly concentrated in the States of Assam, Gujarat, Karnataka, Kerala, Madhya Pradesh, Rajasthan, U.P. and Bihar. These are the States in the Indian Union which have high concentration of Muslim population.

The community has also taken some advantage of Article 30 to establish and manage educational institutions and establish a large network of educational institutions providing secular education with provision of religious education to those students who desire it. These institutions include schools, colleges and even universities. With the advent of privatization of higher education in India during the last one decade, some individuals and trusts/ societies of minority communities including Muslims, have established institutions of professional education under Article 30, offering professional courses in engineering, technology, medicine, dentistry, management and teacher education. But, data indicate that majority of students in such institutions do not belong to the Muslim minority because they are unable to pay the requisite amount of fees which is exorbitantly high. The same thing is true for private schools established by members of Muslim community.

Current Educational Status of Muslims

There is hardly any data-based research report regarding the physical and academic condition of schools in the localities largely inhabited by Muslims. There has been no comprehensive survey on enrolment, dropout rate and learning achievement of Muslim children in two kinds of schooling systems—Madarsa and public. Similarly, scant information in published form is available regarding Muslim youths' overall access to higher education opportunities, participation in professional education, absorption in the employment market and future life accomplishments. However, some minor studies conducted by individuals, government organizations and NGOs here and there, provide some insight into the problems and issues involved in their education. The only authentic government published document now available, which may provide some policy directions, is the much talked about Sachar Committee Report.

A few documents published recently by NUEPA, New Delhi, are useful in getting some idea of the participation of Muslim children in school education (Mehta, 2010). The author has identified 11 States in which Muslim population is more than 10 per cent of the total population of the State and presented a statement of enrolment (per cent) of Muslim children at primary schools stage in comparison to other identified social groups (Table 5.2). It can be observed that while enrolment figures of SC and ST children in all these States (Except Delhi in case of SC) are more than their shares in the total population of the respective States, those of Muslim children are several percentage points below the shares of Muslim population (except in Assam, Karnataka and West Bengal). This shows that Muslim community is educationally backward as

Table 5.2: Primary School Enrolment of Children of Various Social Groups in Selected States

(*per cent*)*

States	*SC*		*ST*		*OBC*		*Muslims*	
	Population	*Enrolment*	*Population*	*Enrolment*	*Population*	*Enrolment*	*Population*	*Enrolment*
Assam	6.90	9.30	12.40	14.60	–	23.20	30.90	35.10
Bihar	15.70	18.20	0.90	2.40	–	60.20	16.50	13.00
Delhi	16.90	11.00	0.00	0.40	–	8.70	11.72	12.30
J&K	7.60	8.50	10.90	15.80	–	8.30	67.00	66.40
Jharkhand	11.80	15.40	26.30	31.70	–	45.40	13.90	10.70
Karnataka	16.20	19.60	6.60	8.10	–	51.90	12.20	14.70
Kerala	9.80	11.60	1.10	2.40	–	63.40	24.70	26.20
Maharashtra	10.20	14.80	8.90	12.80	–	32.30	16.10	9.30
Uttar Pradesh	21.10	27.10	0.10	0.60	–	49.90	18.50	9.60
Uttarakhand	17.90	26.80	3.00	3.30	–	25.50	11.90	13.80
West Bengal	23.00	27.20	5.50	6.70	–	4.70	25.30	28.30
India	**16.20**	**19.90**	**8.20**	**11.70**	–	**42.40**	**13.40**	**11.00**

* Figures compiled from Mehta, 2010.

compared to Scheduled Castes, Scheduled Tribes and Other Backward Classes even at school stage. The situation is more pathetic in the States of Bihar, Delhi, Jharkhand, Uttar Pradesh and Maharashtra where enrolment of Muslim children is less than expected. At the national level, enrolment of Muslim children is 11 per cent compared to 19.9 per cent, 11.7 per cent and 42.4 per cent of SC, ST and OBC children respectively as matched against the share of these groups in the total population of the country.

The situation is equally dismal at the upper primary stage also (Table 5.3). As evident from the given figures, in the case of SC and ST children the enrolment figures are more than their shares in the total population of the respective States (except in Bihar and Delhi for SC children). But, in the case of Muslim children enrolment figures are considerably less than the share of Muslim population in these States (except in Karnataka). At all India level, enrolment figures for SC, ST and OBC children are 19.20 per cent, 9.40 per cent and 41.90 per cent respectively, these are only 9.1 per cent in the case of Muslim children. Even in Kerala which is an educationally advanced State, the enrolment of Muslim children is far below their share in the total population in the State.

When we look at the overall enrolment in elementary schools (classes 1 to 8), we find that the share of Muslim children is 10.5 per cent, while in the case of Scheduled Caste (SC) and Scheduled Tribe (ST) children, the corresponding figures were 19.70 per cent and 11.0 per cent respectively, which are more than their shares of 16.2 per cent and 8.2 per cent respectively in the overall Indian population. Even girls of these sections in the relevant age-group share elementary school enrolment to the extent of 48 per cent of the total enrolment of children coming from these sections.

During the academic session 2006-07, the SC and ST girls enrolled in elementary schools constituted respectively 18.6 per cent and 10.6 per cent of all girls of the same age-group studying in elementary schools (Table 5.4). The OBC girls constitute about 42 per cent of the total enrolment of girls at that stage. Therefore, enrolment of girls belonging to SC, ST and OBC sections is more than their shares in the total population of the country, and thus they are not under-represented. However, in the case of Muslim

Table 5.3: Upper Primary School Enrolment of Children of Various Social Groups in Selected States

(Per cent)

States	SC		ST		OBC		Muslims	
	Population	Enrolment	Population	Enrolment	Population	Enrolment	Population	Enrolment
Assam	6.90	10.80	12.40	16.40	–	26.50	30.90	25.60
Bihar	15.70	13.50	0.90	1.60	–	62.00	16.50	10.30
Delhi	16.90	10.50	0.00	0.30	–	3.10	11.72	10.70
J & K	7.60	8.80	10.90	11.30	–	8.60	67.00	64.00
Jharkhand	11.80	13.00	26.30	27.10	–	48.70	13.90	9.90
Kamataka	16.20	18.30	6.60	7.50	–	53.00	12.20	13.80
Kerala	9.80	11.30	1.10	2.00	–	61.00	24.70	22.00
Maharashtra	10.20	14.60	8.90	9.50	–	32.70	16.10	8.00
Uttar Pradesh	21.10	26.50	0.10	0.50	–	47.00	18.50	7.50
Uttarakhand	17.90	24.70	3.00	3.80	–	18.70	11.90	7.30
West Bengal	23.00	27.80	5.50	5.20	–	8.80	25.30	20.00
India	16.20	19.20	8.20	9.40	–	41.90	13.40	9.10

girls situation is different. Their enrolment is 9.10 per cent of the total enrolment of girls, which is larger than all Muslim children (8.90%) in the elementary school enrolment. This shows that enrolment per cent of Muslim boys is less than that of Muslim girls. This is a matter of special interest and calls for a deeper probe into the situation.

At the secondary education stage (for children aged 14-16 years), enrolment of all girls (2005-06) was 42 per cent of the total enrolment at that stage. While all enrolled SC children constituted about 14.50 per cent of the total enrolment at that stage, SC girls were 39.60 per cent of all SC children and 13.70 per cent of all girls. Similarly, enrolled ST children were 5.70 per cent of all secondary school children and enrolled ST girls were 39.10 per cent of all enrolled ST children. But, enrolled ST girls were only 5.30 per cent of all secondary school girls. The overall situation indicates that both SC and ST children enrolled in secondary schools are slightly less than the shares of these communities in the total population of the country, the situation being more alarming in the case of girls belonging to these sections. The figures for enrolment of Muslim children at secondary stage could not be available.

Traditionally, higher education has been a privilege of affluent classes in all societies. At the time of Independence, only a microscopically small portion of the people had access to higher education institutions. However, during the last six decades there has been noticeable development of higher education system, and now, even some youths from weaker sections have had access to highly specialized professional courses. In the academic year 2004-05, for which data are available (Table 5.5), the gross enrolment ratio (GER) of SCs was 7.8 per cent against 16.7 per cent for youth of non-scheduled general category. Similarly, GERs of STs and OBCs were 7.6 per cent and 10.1 per cent respectively. The GER of women of general category was 14.1 per cent which was more than twice those of SC and ST women, and approximately twice that of OBC women. GERs for women in all social groups have

Table 5.4: Enrolment of Children of Various Social Groups at School Stage (2006-07)

Categories of Children	*Total Enrolment (Millions)*	*Per cent of Total*	*All Girls (Millions)*	*All Girls (Per cent)*
Elementary Stage (Classes 1-8): 2006-07				
All Children	179.30	100.00	85.50	47.70
Rural	143.10	80.00	68.20	47.60
Urban	36.20	20.00	17.30	47.80
Scheduled Castes	35.60	19.90	15.90	44.70 (18.60*)
Scheduled Tribes	19.20	10.70	9.10	47.40 (10.60*)
OBCs	75.20	41.90	35.80	47.60 (41.90*)
Muslim	15.90	8.90	7.80	49.00 (9.10*)
Disabled	1.43	0.80	0.60	42.00 (0.70*)
Secondary Stage (Classes 9-12): 2005-06 *				
All Children	38.40	100.00	16.10	42.00
Scheduled Castes	5.56	14.50	2.20	39.60 (13.70)*
Scheduled Tribes	2.20	5.70	0.86	39.10 (5.30)*

*As per cent of all girls at the corresponding stage.
** Data for Muslim and Disabled girls at secondary stage are not available.
Source: Mehta A.C. (2008): Elementary education in India—Analytical Tables 2006-07, NUEPA, New Delhi.

been lower than their men counterparts across all social, economic, religious and rural-urban groups.

The enrolment figures in higher education in respect of various religious groups are startling in the sense that Muslim community as the largest minority group has the smallest enrolment. While national level GER at higher education stage was more than 12 per cent, it was 19.9 per cent for Christians, 13.1 per cent for Hindus and 12.7 per cent for Sikhs. In the case of Muslims the figure was only 7.7 per cent against their share of 13.4 per cent in the Indian population. In the case of Muslim women the GER was only 6.2 per cent as against 10.9 per cent for Hindu women, 20.0 per cent for Christian women, and 15 per cent for Sikh women.

Table 5.5: Enrolment (per cent) of Youth in Various Higher Education by Various Socio-economic Factors (2004-05)

Factor	*Social Group*	*All*	*Men*	*Women*
Caste Groups	SCs	7.80	9.20	6.30
	STs	7.60	8.80	6.40
	OBCs	10.10	12.50	7.60
	Others	16.70	19.20	14.10
Residence	Rural	7.50	9.30	5.70
	Urban	23.80	24.80	22.60
Poverty	Rich	32.80	33.20	32.30
	Poor	1.60	2.10	1.20
Religion	Hindu	13.10	15.20	10.90
	Muslim	7.70	9.10	6.20
	Sikh	12.70	10.80	15.00
	Christian	19.90	19.70	20.00
	Others	17.70	20.30	14.80
Total	**All groups**	**12.60**	**14.40**	**10.60**

Source: Raju, S. (2008).

Issues and Problems

As mentioned earlier, all minorities other than Muslims have taken care of their educational advancement by reaping full advantage of Constitutional provisions. But, Muslim community somehow could not do so. There is hardly any authentic comprehensive research study to explore the reasons for this state of affairs. While members of the community complain of being discriminated against, others attribute it to the particular ethos of their religion or a minority psychology. It is generally believed that Muslims do not prefer to send their children, especially girls, to government schools. They are mainly concerned about religious education and, therefore, are inclined to open more and more *Maktabs* and *Madarsas*. However, none of these views has a firm empirical base. But, it is true that educational backwardness is at the root of all kinds of socio-economic deprivation. The Muslim intelligentsia attributes it to the absence of true Muslim leadership in the post-Partition period, feeling of insecurity and acute poverty. With the exception of some parts of Kerala, these Madarsas cater strictly to the educational needs of Muslim children. Ever since their emergence, the Madarsas have followed a rigid curriculum providing education to millions of Muslim children only in literature and Islamic studies along with a cursory knowledge of social sciences and other secular subjects. It should be a matter of concern not only to their parents but also to anybody concerned with education in any manner. The format of the education imparted to the students of Madarsas ought to be modified keeping in view the shifting demands of the employers—a concern which can no longer be underplayed. And this is perfectly possible without an erosion of the cultural and religious identity.

Forwarding more of what they are currently doing is not the solution to these problems. To survive present and future challenges, the Madarsas must find new ways to extend contemporary education to their students. Developing suitable answers for today's dilemmas requires an examination of the essentials of education. Education involves transference to others, of knowledge and values accumulated by mankind. Even though schools and teachers have been part of the process of education for hundreds or even thousands of years, it is the spirit of enquiry that has enriched mankind with knowledge. We learn through reading, experience, by watching others and by observing the world in general. Inculcating a spirit of scientific enquiry in students will perhaps be the best manner of propelling them on the path of learning.

In this context it becomes necessary to stress that science education, coupled with modern technology, if put to proper use in Madarsas, could probably make education more meaningful. In modern times, there has been a paradigm shift in the business of education from 'teaching' to 'learning'. It is a demonstrated fact that much learning can happen if the student is left to himself in the proper environment, with the proper resources, tools, and most of all, with proper guidance. Fundamental changes in the educational system may be possible, and indeed essential.

Sometimes it appears that the members of the community are

reluctant to bring about some improvement/change in the pattern of Madarsa's education. Government of India has been toying with the idea of modernization of Madarsa education in the country for the last three years so as to include secular subjects like science and mathematics in addition to the existing religious education. Recently, the Government of India proposed to establish a Madarsa Board for this purpose and convened the meeting of Muslim MPs to discuss the underlying issues and to give a concrete shape to the proposal. About 60 Muslim MPs were invited of which 30 agreed to attend the meeting, but at last, only 18 turned up. Moreover, one-third of the MPs present rejected the idea of setting up a Madarsa Board outright (*Dainik Jagran*, October 4, 2009, page 2). This shows their indifference to the proposal. Disappointed by it, the HRD Minister, Kapil Sibbal, declared that the proposed board will not be created unless Muslim community agrees.

It is accepted that thousands of Madarsas in the country are playing a crucial role in increasing the literacy level of masses, without taking any aid from the government in most cases. While to a degree, certain Madarsas have made a decisive beginning towards modernizing their educational infrastructure, the need of spreading this further was voiced. It was felt, greater importance should be given to taking measures, which boost the morale of the Madarsa Students, pushing their economic aspirations beyond the boundaries of Madarsa-Masjid. Modernization of Madarsas was viewed as a solution to problems as backwardness of Indian Muslims in the field of modern education.

Some prominent members of the community feel that Muslims have four major problems which are the real obstacles in their educational, economic and socio-political advancement. *First,* it is complained that there has been absence of true Muslim leadership in India during the period after partition of the country in 1947. Those who claimed to be leaders of the community were either puppets of the leading political parties to which they belonged or had little understanding and concern for its problems. Unfortunately, they tend to forget the issues concerning their community which votes them to power. But, this is true for all politicians. *Second* major problem is that of security. The members of the community feel that riots and communal violence have been a sad reality of India's life and the majority of the victims of such events have been Muslims. *Third,* it is a proven fact that a large majority of the members of the community live under acute poverty since most of them are involved in low-income vocations or professions. While it is true that the economic and social status of Muslims is not the same throughout India, we cannot deny the fact that poverty and lack of genuine financial resources are hampering their socio-educational development. On the average, they are lower than the members of the majority community on all economic indicators. They are mostly involved in casual labour, and hence, earn less. Consequently, they spend less on items of daily consumption as well as on essential services like education. *Fourth,* they feel that the most painful problem for them is the discriminatory attitude of the majority community towards them in all walks of life.

REFERENCES

Dainik Jagaran (2009): *Sansadon Ki Berukhi Se Phir Atki Madarsah Board Ki Muhim,* Jagaran Bureau, New Delhi, October 4, 2009, page 2.

Ghurye, G.S. (1969): *Caste and Race in India,* Popular Prakashan, Bombay.

Government of India (2008): Selected Educational Statistics, MHRD, New Delhi.

Mehta, A.C. (2010): Elementary Education in India—Progress towards UEE (DISE 2008-09), NUEPA, New Delhi.

Raju, S. (2008): Gender Differentials in Access to Higher Education, in *Higher Education in India—Issues related to Expansion, Inclusiveness, Quality and Finance,* University Grants Commission, New Delhi.

Shah, S. Shamim, *Educational Survey Report on Muslim Managed Schools and Colleges in India,* Hamdard Education Society, New Delhi, 1983.

Srinivas, M.N. (1962): *Caste in Modern India and Other Essays,* Asia Publishing House, Bombay.

6

Muslim Managed Degree Colleges : How to Revitalize These ?

A.R. Kidwai

Although the exact number of Muslim Managed or Minority Colleges (MMDCs) is not known, there are at least 400-500 of these colleges across the country. In 1999, when I was the Director of Centre for Promotion of the Cultural and Educational Advancement of Muslims of India, Aligarh Muslim University, an empirical study, though at a modest scale, was carried out in order to formulate a profile of these colleges. Accordingly an extensive questionnaire was circulated. It elucidated concrete information about the academic, administrative and financial profile of these colleges. Some of the key questions were:

- The number of students.
- The faculty-wise enrolment of the students.
- The provision for postgraduate courses.
- The performance of students.
- The professional qualifications of teachers.
- The provision for technical or professional courses.
- The financial status of these colleges.

Empirical data were obtained from 92 colleges while partial informations could be gained about another 79 colleges.

The Ground Realities

The following points merit attention in the light of the data provided by these colleges:

- Only 20 per cent of these MMDCs have provision for teaching science subjects.
- Only 21 per cent of these offer Research facilities.
- Only 40 per cent of these have postgraduate teaching.
- Only 33 per cent of these provide Professional/Job Oriented Courses.
- Only 40 per cent of these have more than 1,000 students on roll.
- Only 40 per cent of the staff of these possess Ph.D.
- Only 30 per cent of these have three Faculties.
- Only 40 per cent of these have more than 10,000 titles in their College Library.

Some other significant pointers:

- 50 per cent of these came into existence in 1970s onwards.
- Only 20 per cent of these are for girls while 72 per cent are co-educational.
- Only 13 per cent of these admit students through Entrance Test while 87 per cent do so on the basis of marks in the qualifying examination.
- 34 per cent of these have less than 50 per cent Muslim students.

As is evident from the above, much needs to be done for revitalizing these colleges so that they may contribute meaningfully to the H.E. sector.

A Possible Remedy

Over the years the Academic Staff Colleges have been hub of in-service training and Orientation Programmes which are geared towards the professional development of University/College teachers. These colleges provide an opportunity for college teachers to gain effective skills of teaching, educational technology and personality development. These seek to sensitize teachers to the linkages between education and economic, socio-economic and cultural development. These also help them appreciate the organization and management of College and University and to pursue the role of teachers in the total system. Another laudable feature of Academic Staff College courses is that these help teachers recognize the nuances of the Indian polity, of which the basic tenets are: democracy, secularism, equal opportunities and gender justice. Both during and after attending the Academic Staff College courses teachers are much better placed to perceive and reflect on the meaningful role of teachers in both their respective institutions and in the broader community life. These courses go a long way in bringing about the personality development of teachers and induce among them initiative, creativity and leadership. Equipped with Computer Laboratories the Academic Staff Colleges have played a major role also in promoting computer literacy and the use of ICT in teaching and learning process.

The establishment of a *Nodal Agency* for the revitalization for the Muslim Managed Degree Colleges at the Aligarh Muslim University might help improve the quality of these colleges. As the Aligarh Muslim University Act of 1920, as amended in 1981 has entrusted the AMU with the responsibility to work for the promotion of the education and cultural advancement for Muslims of India, the UGC Academic Staff College at the AMU is suited best for its role as the *Nodal Agency* for the quality improvement of these colleges. Since 1987, the UGC Academic Staff College, Aligarh Muslim University has been organizing Orientation Programmes and Subject Refresher Courses. The range of its activities is:

Orientation Programmes	:	107
Subject Refresher Courses	:	314
No. of University Colleges teachers who have benefited from these courses	:	12,000

Plan of Action

The proposed Nodal Agency will take up the following:

(i) To conduct a detailed survey of all the MMDCs along the above lines with the help of Questionnaires/Field work/ On the spot visits.

(ii) The MMDC staff will be provided training, covering the following components:
   (a) Motivation/sensitization;
   (b) Personality development;
   (c) Awareness of the opportunities (UGC/Government of India Schemes for Minorities and for Job-Oriented Courses);
   (d) Quality assurance programmes;
   (e) Communication skills;
   (f) Teaching skills;
   (g) Academic and research skills;
   (h) Awareness of linkages between education and industry;
   (i) Staff Development Courses; and
   (j) Awareness of quality benchmarks.

Orientation Programmes, Workshops, Interactive Sessions will be organized by the Nodal Agency both at AMU, Aligarh and at its regional centres across the country.

What are the Benefits of the Nodal Agency ?

The proposed courses by the *Nodal Agency* will accrue the following benefits for MMDCs:

Re-Engineering the Academic Climate of MMDCs

- Overall academic development of these colleges.
- Professional training of their staff members.
- Quality improvement in these colleges.
- Introduction of Job Oriented Courses.
- Better teaching methodology and skills.

- Management skills.
- Orientation of students of challenges of life.
- Making their staff and students better citizens.
- Gaining the latest knowledge about Information Technology.
- Training their staff and students as agents of socio-economic reform and change and national development.

In brief, it is bound to transform the existing scenario.

For achieving the above objectives the *NODAL AGENCY* at AMU Academic Staff College proposes to organize Orientation Programme/Workshops/Interactive Sessions in the following broad areas:

- Academic/Research skills.
- Securing UGC scheme/funds for Academic Projects.
- Communication Skills.
- Management Skills.
- Educational technology Awareness.
- Information technology Training.
- Professional/Job Oriented Courses.
- Personality Development Skills.
- Nation Building and National Integration Drives.
- National Development Programmes.
- Testing and Evaluation Practices.
- Academic Administration.
- Quality Assurance Programme.

Proposed Functioning of the Nodal Agency

The Nodal Agency, AMU Academic Staff College will function on the pattern of the UGC Academic Staff College (in terms of its Functions/Structure and Financial powers of the Director, Opening of Bank Accounts/Registration Fee/Assets and Liabilities) as stipulated in the Eleventh Plan UGC Guidelines for Academic Staff College.

The Academic Advisory Committee may comprise the following:

(a) Vice Chancellor, AMU (Chairman);
(b) HRD Nominee;
(c) UGC Nominee;
(d) Two Managers of MMDCs;
(e) Two Principals of MMDCs;
(f) Two Eminent Educationists;
(g) Two Representation of NGOs engaged in the promotion of education among Muslims;
(h) Director, AMU Academic Staff College (Secretary);
(i) Registrar and Finance Officer, AMU will be special invitees;
(j) All members except (b) and (c) will be nominated by Chairman in consultation with the Director, UGC Academic Staff College, Aligarh Muslim University;
(k) The Committee will meet twice a year; and
(l) All matters relating to the *Nodal Agency*, including financial matters will be placed before the Committee.

7

Empowerment of Muslims in the Twelfth Five Year Plan (2012-17)

Mohd. Muzammil

The focus of the Eleventh Five Year Plan has been on 'inclusive growth'. The proposed goal of the Twelfth Five Year Plan is: "Faster, Sustainable and More Inclusive Growth." The agenda naturally demands inclusion of the excluded sections of the population. Inclusion of minorities particularly Muslims in the mainstream of economic development would be an important agenda of the developmental efforts in the ensuing Five Year Plan. According to Sachar Committee Report, Muslims are the poorest and least empowered minority in India.

As per the proposed approach, the Twelfth Plan will cover these five areas:

- The Goal: Faster, Sustainable and More Inclusive Growth;
- Macro framework: Sustaining high growth, price stability, Saving and Investment, BoP and Budget balancing;
- The People: Education, health, faster expansion of jobs, skill development and social justice—empowering the excluded;
- The Planet: Climate change, water, forests, energy; and
- Making it happen: Good governance, innovation and science in all sectors, reducing inequality.

For empowering Muslims in the Plan period, we can suggest to have a national and a sub-national Muslim Empowerment Measure

(MEM) that needs to concentrate on three points: (i) economic empowerment, (ii) professional empowerment, and (iii) political empowerment.

Power on economic resources can be increased by enabling the Muslim community to have higher per capita income which can be taken as the variable for economic empowerment. Professional empowerment can be accomplished by increasing the access of Muslims to professional opportunities and participation in decision making—enabling them to lead a fuller, richer and more varied life. Professional empowerment can be ensured by enhancing their share in four areas of regular employment (i) professional jobs, (ii) technical jobs, (iii) administrative jobs, and (iv) managerial jobs.

Access to political opportunities of the Muslim community needs to be ensured in the proportion of their share in population. This can be done by seeing to it that they have access to seats/adequate representation in the (a) national Parliament, (b) State Assemblies, and (c) at the local level Punchayati Raj Institutions in rural and urban areas.

The per capita income (adjusted to purchasing power) is the outcome of employment opportunities. And employment of Muslims have been surrounded by a plethora of problems. Addressing these barriers and reducing all sorts of discrimination would help them have gainful employment, decent work and better jobs.

The National Five Year Plan looks at the country as a whole. It also needs to have regional and State perspective with a view to empower Muslims. Muslims are in majority in the UT of Lakshadweep and in the State of Jammu and Kashmir. In other six States the proportion of Muslims is higher than the national average. These States are: Assam, West Bengal, Kerala, Uttar Pradesh, Bihar and Jharkhand. Specific empowerment measures will be required in these States.

The Twelfth Five Year Plan of these States must run in close coordination with the central Plan strategy for empowering Muslims. These States' Twelfth Five Year Plan must aim at achieving the Plan targets set by the Central Plan.

Employment is closely linked with the status of education. Muslim students do not have access to quality education. If education is poor, labour market outcome is also poor. Generally Muslims end up with low paid jobs and less remunerative employment like street vending. In this case, the ratio of Muslim workers is far above the national average.

The provision of reservation appears to have adversely affected employment position of Muslim community. The reason is simple. While 22.2 per cent of the Hindu population is under SC Category only, 0.8 per cent Muslims come under this head. Similarly, while 9 per cent of the Hindus are classified as ST only, 0.5 per cent Muslims belong to this group. Even in the OBC category, where the ratio is substantial even in Muslim community, it is still lower (39.2%) as compared to the ratio of OBC in the Hindu community (42.8%). That is why there have been demands for separate reservation to the Muslim community. The distribution of different categories of religion/caste-wise population shows the dominance of 'general category' among the Muslims to the order of about 60 per cent as compared to 26 per cent for Hindus.

There are 'knowledge gaps' and 'lack of information' in the Muslim community. In the field of bare literacy rate, it is very low among Muslims much below than the national average.

Economic backwardness is often the result of educational deprivation. The low literacy level of Muslims is well documented in various research studies. The condition of Muslims in education is not much different from that of the Scheduled Caste and Scheduled Tribe communities. If the SC/ST and Muslims are excluded, the remaining category of 'Others' would show a high literacy level of 71 per cent.

Health Status of Muslim community presents a dubious situation. While the Body Mass Index (BMI) of Muslim women is better than that of their counterparts in other communities, Muslims have very high rate of underweight children and high child mortality rate. This suggests that the health of women is not reflected into the health of their children. Sex ratio is the best among Muslims (950 women per 1000 men) as compared to other community groups and the national average. Specific measures need to be taken in the next Plan for child care and their general health protection.

The general condition of Muslims in India is causing concern although all is not dark and depressing. The plus points need to be capitalised to promote them in other areas of development. The position in case of demographic indicators is not depressing. But the educational scenario is bleak indeed. Economic status is really poor and work participation rate has serious gaps both in rural and urban areas. Muslims remain grossly underrepresented in public services. They often suffer from what is called: 'double discrimination being Muslim and being poor'.

There is a need for an integrated approach of educational, social and economic development of Muslims. In a model that I suggested much earlier in 1992, it was advocated that micro models of upliftment would work better than macro policy measures.

Further, the educational needs of the lower and middle class Muslim families are different from those of the rich class of the same community. The role of the government and the Muslim leadership is more important for the general community. In the Twelfth Five Year Plan, ensuring universal elementary education along the Muslim children will go a long way in helping India achieve the First of the Millennium Development Goals (i.e., achieving universal primary education) by 2015. Promotion of good quality secondary and higher education along with vocational and managerial specialization would be very helpful in educational upliftment and empowerment.

A suitably designed strategic mechanism needs to be found out for educational advancement and larger entry of Muslim students in the IIMs and IITs and top universities and colleges of the country. As of now, only one out of 25 UG and 50 PG students in premier colleges is a Muslim.

Enhancing the enrolment in professional and managerial education may lead to a real breakthrough in the vicious circle of illiteracy and poverty that plagues the Muslim community in India. Muslim intellectuals need to be proactive and come out to provide the real leadership to this community as the existing political captaincy of the community has been very weak which miserably failed to prevail upon the government for adopting developmental policies for this group. They would also be capable of seeing that religious instruction does not come in the way of educational awakening and socio-economic modernisation of the Muslim community in general and Muslim women in particular.

Points for consideration in framing the Twelfth Five Year Plan:

- With successively increasing growth rate of the Indian economy from the Sixth Five Year Plan onwards reaching to a growth rate of 8-9 per cent in the Eleventh Plan period, the situation of Muslims has not improved much. The reason is that the link between high growth rate and development of all sections of the society is *not automatic*. High growth rates often failed to benefit the people in many countries.
- External environment favourable to growth is vital for the development of minorities. Peaceful international environment and cordial relations with neighbouring countries would help in promoting schemes of social justice.
- Redirecting Plan allocations and restructuring Plan expenditures can help finance activities that produce better results for minorities. It is often the absence of political will and NOT always the lack of financial resources that is responsible for human neglect.
- Business, trade and financial opportunities without any bias and discrimination can be of greater help than *aid and support* programmes for minorities.
- People's participation is vital. Muslims participation, therefore, needs to be ensured in decisions and processes that shape their own lives.
- Human security is of utmost value. The security of Muslims in their homes, in their business and jobs, in their localities and in their environments with their cultural identities should be of most prime concern. Adam Smith has said: if

a choice is to be made between security and opulence then security is to be preferred.

- Five Year Plan programmes have touched many issues but *not focused* on them. Four critical elements of development: viz., equity, efficiency, sustainability and empowerment demand that minorities' issues be addressed as development issues and human rights issues. Let us give this slogan to the Twelfth Five Year Plan makers in the Planning Commission: *Development if not Minority Rendered is Endangered.*

8

Developing English Language Teacher Training Programme and Enhancing Student Performance in Madarsas located in Muslim Concentration Districts of U.P. and Bihar

Raashid Nehal

Introduction

If we look at the data related to allocation of resources for minorities, the per capita plan allocation of resources for minorities in 2010-11 is Rs. 792 which was even below ST (Rs. 1,521) and SC (Rs. 1,220). Religious minorities including Muslims constitute 19 per cent of the population whereas budgetary allocations for schemes designed for this section is not more than 5 per cent of total plan allocation (Mander, 2011:3, *The Hindu*). According to 2001 Census the all-India literacy rate is 65 per cent, while the functional literacy of Muslims is 59 per cent and it is affected by factors related to poor education coverage. Though only 4 per cent Indian Muslim children attend Madarsas, dismal level of access to English language learning and training opportunities has been a serious factor for the poor education coverage. Today Madarsas across the country provide free education to the poor Muslims. According to a study, around 36 per cent of all school age children in the age group of 6-18 years have been found to be studying in Madarsas in India. Moreover, of those who seek enrolment in Madarsas, only 22 per cent of boys and 17 per cent of girls and 20 per cent of total students manage to reach up to class VIII. (Fahimuddin, cited in Khan *et al.*, 2003:14). Employment generation is also low since only 4 per cent of Indian Muslim children attend Madarsas grow up to become Imams of mosques, teachers and preachers (Sachar Committee Report, 2006). The literacy rate among Muslim girls have improved due to Madarsas in rural India whereas in some Madarsas like in Bihar, are funded by the government and their certificates are valid while applying for jobs (Wajihuddin, 2011). As Madarsas are an increasingly important part of the Indian national education system, the focus of the project proposal is on training teachers to acquire communication skills and to teach English in Maktabs and Madarsas in 28 Muslim concentration districts identified in Uttar Pradesh and Bihar.

Rationale

The objective of the English language curriculum is to encourage traditional institutions like Maktabs and Madarsas to strengthen the teaching of English along with other subjects such as Science, Mathematics, Social Studies, Hindi so as to provide opportunities to students to acquire education comparable to the national system of education (Khan *et al.*, 2003: 25) and to produce high quality graduates who can contribute to national development. It is in this light, Madarsas need to revise and update their syllabi: they need to integrate contemporary knowledge with religious education. Hamid says, 'adoption of modern teaching methods that aim at developing a child's personality and vision will itself generate a demand for review of curriculum (cited in the *Times of India*, 2005: Editor Page). Several strategies have been identified by various commissions and reports constituted by Government of India to address these concerns and to raise the status of Madarsa education. The first is the emphasis on providing need-based and area-specific teacher training with a view to raising the Madarsa student examination scores. This will raise the status of Madarsa education and place Madarsa graduates on an equal footing with graduates of general schools.

Recently, a few Madarsas have incorporated secular subjects like English and Computer Science in their curricula, and in some Madarsa students also do web designing. However, there exists wide disparities in resources allocated for Madarsas between regions and between public and private Madarsa resulting in a lower standard of quality than general schools. Teacher education in Madarsa and student performance in English are basically dependent on the following set of teacher-training activities :

(a) Subject content upgrades and classroom methodologies training;
(b) Training teachers to design and produce need-based ELT materials;
(c) On-going teacher support and mentoring;
(d) Student remedial programmes; and
(e) Upgrade essential teaching/learning resources and facilities.

Impact

Equal access of Madarsas graduates to higher education and to formal sector employment.

Outputs and Interventions

Quality improvement efforts in Madarsas are to be aimed toward the following primary results:

1. To enhance the equity and coverage of Teacher Education in Madarsa within the framework of the National Teacher Education system,
2. To improve the quality of Madarsa teacher as measured by National benchmarks for teacher education quality,
3. To expand opportunities for Teacher education in coming from targeted MCDs poor, rural, remote and disadvantaged areas,
4. Improvement in student's English achievement, and

5. To bring the learner at par with the national mainstream minimum levels of achievement as envisaged by national or State Board.

Scope/Coverage of the English Language Teacher Training Project

(a) Teachers of Primary, Upper Primary and Secondary Schools of Madarsas in 28 Muslim Concentration Districts (MCDs) from UP and Bihar [see list of Minority Concentration Districts (MCDs) under Annexure 1(A). The coverage of the teacher training programme will be extended to teachers Madarsas/Maktabs which are supported under SSA interventions in coordination with State project directorates as well as those other volunteering Madarsas/ Maktabs which may not be registered or recognised under SSA interventions. Sarva Shiksha Abhiyan (SSA) addresses issues of **access, equity and quality.** The findings of the Sachar Committee point out that Muslim children in the age group of 6-14 have either never attended school or have dropped out and also majority of Muslim girls and boys fail in their Matriculation examination or they drop out.

(b) Teachers imparting vocational training in 28 MCDs under the scheme of Jan Shikshan Sansthan (JSSs). Skill development may be relevant for those who have not completed school education.

Approach and Methodology

Top down approaches to the development of education have proven ineffective in many instances. Target area-based planning approaches with community involvement have proven more effective in identifying real needs for quality improvement. The project design is based on a "whole Madarsa", cluster approach. This approach involves concentrating support on a local network (cluster) of Madarsa and responding to the development priorities identified by the Madarsa themselves. A participatory Madarsa development process will be used by each Madarsa to identify its priorities for English language quality improvement. Through this participatory process, madarsa principals and teachers, with their local communities, Madarsa committees, and leadership identify priorities for the development of as a whole. The priorities under the proposed project will include detailed reports on giving suggestions relating to upgrading under-qualified or mismatched teachers, learning materials provision, facilities upgrading, provision of English language centres, and/or addition of libraries, and IT facilities. In addition, the use of international consultants *versus* local trainers is very expensive given the need for ongoing guidance, support, and capacity building. Also, it makes it difficult to develop a local cadre of experts who can provide ongoing support to capacity building. A cadre of locally-based advisors, facilitators and/or trainers, trained by national and international experts, provide a more sustainable local resource network.

The Government of India major flagship programme Muslim-Sectoral Development identifies 90 districts in which Muslims are 25 per cent or more of the population. 28 MCDs are selected from UP and Bihar that have been identified below the national socio-economic parameters. This is because Muslim settlements have few government schools and those that exist lack of facilities and staff. The project is thus an attempt to investigate issues on a separate budgetary sub-plan for making investments exclusively for MCDs based Madarsa teachers in 28 identified districts of U.P. and Bihar developing English communication skills programme for the selected MCDs will help reduce imbalances and disparities. Priority will be given to such pockets in each MCD that focus on villages, blocks and localities having a substantial disadvantaged minority population. The focus of the project development will be on "development deficits" from U.P. and Bihar districts. The project would be also applicable to those areas having concentration of minority population, with low female literacy and/or a large number of girls out of schools so as to increase female literacy and reduce the gender gap in rural areas, particularly in disadvantaged community. Schools beyond primary level are few in Muslim localities and exclusive schools for girls are fewer (Sachar Committee, 2006).

As regards the logistics of this project is concerned, NGO will be entrusted to complete surveys of 28 MCDs for making District-level plans for upgrading teacher education. Workshop will be developed to reach Madarsa administrators/principals from the cluster of Madarsa at local level. The workshop will:

(i) review training needs, propose training activities and schedules for review by a respective Madarsa,
(ii) prepare a training manual for the approved training programmes,
(iii) develop, trial and revise the manual,
(iv) conduct national training for trainers,
(v) prepare and produce training materials,
(vi) implement, monitor and evaluate the training activities, and
(vii) conduct regional and national workshop as follow-up and improve future training programmes.

Each of 28 MCD Madarsa district involved in the Project will prepare a three-year Madarsa development plan prior to the end of the first year of project implementation. The plans will identify activities and resource requirements and investment plans for language development programme of the Madarsa.

Improving Quality of Madarsa Education

A.1. Improve Teacher Professionalism and Student Performance

A.1.1. Upgrading of MCD/Madarsa Teachers so as to Gain Equal Footing in Professional Certification

Target teachers: 500—year 1

- Development of Instructional materials—1

A.1.2. *Provide Short-Term Training in Subject Content and Classroom Communication Skills*

- 28 of MCD/Madarsa cluster plans for teacher support produced activities.
- Development of Instructional materials—2.

A.1.3. *Provide Madarsa-Based On-Going Teacher Support and Mentoring*

- Number of innovations resulting from innovation grants that are successfully introduced into classrooms.
- Refinement and printing of Instructional materials—3.

A.1.4. *Increase Completion Rates and Examination Pass Rates through the Provision of Student Remedial Programmes*

- Development of Remedial materials.
- Review and revision of Remedial materials.
- Target teachers to be trained in remediation.

B.1. ***Upgrade Essential Teaching/Learning Resources and Facilities***

- Procurement of approved textbooks and learning support materials library and reading materials prepared.
- Rehabilitate and construct required learning facilities.
- Upgrading of furnitures and teaching aids in classrooms.

REFERENCES

Fahimuddin. Globalization and Growth of Madarsas in India.http://www.bsos.umd.edu/socy/conference/newspapers/uddin.txt.

Khan, Amirullah, Md. Saquib and Zafar H. Anjum. 2003. To Kill the Mockingbird Madarsa System in India: Past, Present and Future.< www.indiachina centre.org/bazaar./pdfs/madarsas.pdf

Mander, Harsh. (2011). 'if we walk together'. *The Hindu* Sunday, March 13, p. 3.

National Curriculum Framework. 2005. NCERT, New Delhi.

Rahmani, Md. Wali. (2009). Minority Concentrated Districts' Development Plan, Government Charter and Muslim Point of View. Rahmani Foundation. Kanquah Rahmani. Munger.

Sachar Committee Report. 2006. Government of India.

The Times of India (2005). 'Should Madarsa Curriculum be modernised' Editorial November 20, p. 16.

Wajihuddin, Mohd. (2011). Allah ke Bande. *The Times of India*, the Crescent Edition. Saturday, February 19, p. 8.

ANNEXURE I(A)

List of Districts selected from UP and Bihar having Socio-Economic and/or Basic Amenities below National Average

Sr. No.	Sub-group Sl. No.	States	Districts
1.	30	Uttar Pradesh	Bulandshahar
2.	31	Uttar Pradesh	Badaun
3.	32	Uttar Pradesh	Barabanki
4.	33.	Uttar Pradesh	Kheri
5.	34.	Uttar Pradesh	Shajahanpur
6.	35.	Uttar Pradesh	Moradabad
7.	36	Uttar Pradesh	Rampur
8.	37	Uttar Pradesh	Jyotiba Phule Nagar
9.	38	Uttar Pradesh	Bareilly
10.	39	Uttar Pradesh	Pilibhit
11.	40	Uttar Pradesh	Bahraich
12.	41	Uttar Pradesh	Shrawasti
13.	42	Uttar Pradesh	Balrampur
14.	43	Uttar Pradesh	Siddharthnagar
15.	44	Uttar Pradesh	Bijnor
16.	17	Bihar	Araria
17.	18	Bihar	Kishanganj
18.	19	Bihar	Pumia
19.	20	Bihar	Katihar
20.	21	Bihar	Sitamarhi
21.	22	Bihar	Paschim Champaran
22.	23	Bihar	Darbhanga
23.	10	Uttar Pradesh	Lucknow
24.	11	Uttar Pradesh	Saharanpur
25.	12	Uttar Pradesh	Meerut
26.	13	Uttar Pradesh	Muzzaffarnagar
27.	14	Uttar Pradesh	Baghpat
28.	15	Uttar Pradesh	Ghaziabad

ANNEXURE I(B)

FINANCIAL ESTIMATES—I

Scenario I: Cost Estimates for 20 Teachers and 100 Students

Cost per annum: Based on calculations for 20 teachers and 100 students. The number of students/teachers can, however, increase. The unit cost excludes the cost incurred on infrastructure. [upgrading, renovating and building classrooms, toilets, library and other facilities]

S. No.	*Item of Expenditure*	*Rs. in lakhs 1 Unit Cost:20 Teachers: 100 Students*
1.	1 -4 weeks Refresher Course for 20 teachers	1.5 lakh
	• Short-term Teacher Training Workshops [see A.1.1]	
	• Consultancy Charges	1.0 lakh
2.	Course books, teaching aids, stationery and other Educational material @ Rs. 50 per month	0.60
3.	Preparation of English Language Teaching learning/Instructional material	3.00
	Development of Remedial materials	
4.	Equipment and Software	0.40
	Library Books	0 .40
5.	1 Course Coordinator—Honorarium	0.50
6.	3 Support staff – 2 (Accountant/Assistant) –1 Peon	
	Miscellaneous including maintenance and Hiring Services [photocopying, printing, contingency]	0.60
	Telephone charges, internet charges, fax	
	Total cost	Rs 8.0 lakh per unit cost

9

Empowerment of Minorities through Equalization of Opportunities: Some Tentative Suggestions

Md. Zafar Mahfooz Nomani

I. Sociological Context of Muslim Problem

The Studies on Muslims in India are generally explored out of politicization of Hindu-Muslim relationship and channelizing to vote bank politics.[1] This trivializes access, empowerment and equalization of opportunities enshrined in the Constitution.[2] The Right to Equality goes beyond a formal requirement of ensuring absence of direct discrimination and puts a positive obligation on the State to control direct as well as indirect discrimination, eliminate extreme forms of deprivation and take into account the burden of history. The sense of siege is visible in lethal way in their presence in prison indeed a good index of discrimination against Muslims. In Gujarat, Muslims are two and half-times likelier to be a prison than Hindus in relation to their population. In Maharashtra, Muslims, account for 10.4 per cent of the population, but for 40.6 per cent of all prisoners. In Tamil Nadu 5.6 per cent Muslims but 9.6 per cent Muslim prisoners. More than 60 per cent of this prison population consists of under trials. They are probable victims of the selective recent application of anti-terrorist measures to Muslims. The stereotyping of Muslim problems are centred around bland and banal descriptions in social structure,[3] sociological and anthropological study on caste among

Muslims,[4] sociological and anthropological study of Muslims,[5] and interaction of Muslim such as on the approach to the study of Islam in south Asia.[6] The Muslim studies require a dispassionate reading of contemporary history to locate causes the process of social exclusion and inclusion[7] leading to the present states of the Muslims and understanding for the appropriateness of corrective measures.

II. Access to Education of Muslim

The illiteracy is the root cause of social exclusion of Muslims in India.[8] The prerequisite of the empowerment is access to education. Education, an important indicator of social inclusion[9] and human development, merits attention to understand the Muslim position on the basis of data collected by some sample surveys, Massey (1998) concludes that the literacy level among the Muslims is on an average 10 per cent less than the National level.[10] While National Commission for Minorities finds that the enormous Muslim population is terribly under-represented in all public services.[11] According to the 2001 Census, Muslims literacy rate is 59 per cent as against the national average of 65 per cent. It is lower than OBC but higher than SCs and STs who together record 53 per cent literacy. Muslims have a higher literacy rate than the State average in many States like, Kerala, Jharkhand, Karnataka, Maharashtra, Andhra Pradesh, etc. State average in all northern States, not only in the BIMARU State but also in developed ones like Delhi, Punjab and Haryana and western Uttar Pradesh. More than 1,000 Muslim concentrated village in West Bengal, Bihar and U.P. do not have any educational institutions. The situation is worse in villages with smaller Muslim concentrations. There is more disparity in graduate attainment rate between Muslim and other categories and it has been widening since 1990s in both urban as well as rural areas. Only one out of 25 undergraduate students and only one out of 50 post-graduates students in premier college, are Muslims pursuing post-graduation is lower among Muslims than other socio-religious communities (SRCs) among Hindus general it is 29 per cent, SCs and STs 28 per cent, OBCs 23 per cent and Muslim 16 per cent.

Table 9.1: Literacy and Enrolment Rate by Population Groups

Social Groups	*Literacy Rate (7 yrs and above)*			*Gender disparity in Literacy*	*Ever Enrolment Rate (6-14) years*			*Gender disparity in Enrolment*
	Persons	Male	Female		Persons	Male	Female	
Caste								
STs	39.3	51.4	26.0	0.51	60.3	67.6	51.5	0.76
SCs	41.5	53.4	28.2	0.53	62.5	69.6	54.7	0.79
Religion								
Hindus	53.3	65.9	39.2	0.59	72.0	78.1	65.1	0.83
Muslims	49.4	59.5	38.0	0.64	61.6	66.2	56.6	0.85
Christians	80.8	85.0	76.5	0.90	91.3	90.7	92.1	1.02
Other Minorities	53.8	62.9	43.8	0.70	78.5	83.2	73.6	0.88

Source: India Human Development Report, 1999.

The educational policies after independence have been perceived by Muslims in India to be a threat to their identity resulted their preference to send their children to traditional centres of education. This perhaps could be an important reason for increase in the number of Muslim managed educational institutions. The NCAER data shows that while 70.3 per cent of Hindu children in the age group of 6-14 years go to government schools, the percentage of Muslim children going to government schools is only 49.5 per cent.[12] Table 9.1 presents the levels of literacy of 7+ population revealing the literacy rate is low (49%) among Muslims in comparison to Hindu (53%), Christians (81%) and other minorities (54%).

The universalisation of elementary education among Muslims must be effectively and immediately introduced. The schooling facilities for Muslim by way of constitutional commitment of Articles 29 and 30 of Constitution in Muslim concentration areas considered to be affront to majority community. The Maktabs and Madarsas, in their courses of study did not facilitate their entry into so called mainstream education.

III. Share in Employment

The educational backwardness of Muslims led to minimum opportunity and participation[13] which is tabulated under Table 9.2:

Table 9.2: Pattern of Employment by Religion in India

Residence/ Sex & Religion	*Self-employed*	*Regular Workers*	*Casual Workers*	*All*	*WPR*
Urban Males					
Hindus	39.1	46.4	14.5	100.0	52.0
Muslims	53.3	29.9	16.7	100.0	49.1
Christians	29.7	53.4	17.0	100.0	48.1
Urban Females					
Hindus	45.0	27.7	26.4	100.0	15.9
Muslims	60.0	15.7	24.3	100.0	11.4
Christians	34.3	51.5	14.2	100.0	23.6
Rural Males					
Hindus	58.5	10.1	31.4	100.0	54.2
Muslims	59.0	7.5	33.5	100.0	50.5
Christians	52.1	12.0	35.9	100.0	—
Rural Females					
Hindus	59.9	3.6	36.5	100.0	33.7
Muslims	67.9	3.0	29.1	100.0	19.6
Christians	57.6	9.9	32.4	100.0	37.3

Source: NSS 43rd Round, 1987-88 cited in Abusaleh Shariff, *EPW*, November 18, 1995.

Nearly half of Muslim men between the ages 25 and 45 are self employed as compared to 28 per cent of *dalit*. Only 18 per cent are regular employment as compared to 25 per cent of Hindus. Muslims have under-representation in Government jobs as evident from the data compiled by the Sachar Committee Report[14] from 12 States tabulated as under Table 9.3.

In all the States the representation of Muslims in government service is far below their proportion on the population.[15] The notable exception in Andhra Pradesh. There representation of Muslims in Government service is about same as their proportion in population. The Muslims in Indian elite cadre service have no change. Such as Indian Administrative Service (IAS) (3.1%), the Indian Foreign Service (IFS) (1.8%), and the Indian Police Service (IPS) (4%). Muslims are altogether barred from key "line" positions

Table 9.3 : Muslim Representation in Employment in India

Sl. No.	Name of State	Muslims % of Population in States	% of Muslims Share in State Employment
1.	Assam	30.9	11.2
2.	Kerala	24.7	10.4
3.	West Bengal	25.0	4.2
4.	Karnataka	12.2	8.5
5.	Tamil Nadu	5.6	3.2
6.	Uttar Pradesh	18.5	5.1
7.	Bihar	16.5	7.6
8.	Maharashtra	10.6	4.4
9.	Delhi	11.7	3.2
10.	Gujarat	9.1	5.6
11.	Andhra Pradesh	9.2	8.8
12.	Jharkhand	13.8	6.7

Source: Sachar Committee Report, 2006, p. 370.

in the intelligence agencies, the Indian Space Research Organization, National Security Guards and other VVIP protection forces. Their presence in paramilitary forces is nominal (1 to 3%), in the armed forces Muslim representation is only 2 per cent.

IV. Representation in Politics

In political field too Muslim never got representations in proportion to their population. The number of MPs did not even reach 10 per cent in any elected Parliament.[16] It is even worse when it comes to State assemblies.

Iqbal Ansari who has given a detailed account of political exclusion. In his book "Political Representation of Muslims in India 1952-2004", for the Lok Sabha and 12 State assemblies, including the six States (U.P., West Bengal, Bihar, Assam, Maharashtra and Kerala). The number of Muslim Lok Sabha M.Ps has varied between 21 and 49 or between just 4.3 and 6.6 per cent of the strength of the House. The number reached 40 plus only in the seventh and eighth Lok Sabhas (1980 and 1984) in 2004 and it has now fallen to 36. The average for the last three Lok Sabha is just 6 per cent.[17] The political participation rate is depicted in Sidiqui's work and tabulated under Table 9.4.

Muslim exclusions or under-representation in the Lok Sabha

Table 9.4: Political Participation Rate of Muslims in India

Year	*Total*	*No. of Muslims in Lok Sabha*	*Percentage of Muslim Legislators*
1952	489	23	4.49
1957	494	22	4.65
1962	494	22	4.45
1967	520	29	5.75
1971	518	29	5.59
1977	542	33	6.08
1980	542	49	9.04
1984	543	45	8.28
1989	543	33	6.07
1991	543	28	5.15
1996	543	27	4.97

Source: M.K. Siddiqui (Ed.), *Muslims in Free India*, p. 41.

is measured in relation to their population. As it stands 47.12 per cent from 1952-2004. It is high in Rajasthan (91%), Delhi (86%), Gujarat (82%), Maharashtra (72%), M.P. (50%), Tamil Nadu (53%). Even in West Bengal and Kerala, with a strong Muslim population but deprivation is more than 40 per cent. In the State Legislative Assembly, the deprivation is even more dismal. In Andhra Pradesh Legislative Assembly 61 per cent, Bihar 47 per cent, Gujarat 79 per cent, Karnataka 71 per cent, Madhya Pradesh 69 per cent, Maharashtra 62 per cent, and in U.P. 47 per cent. The primary reason for Muslim under-representation is their under-nominated by political parties. In the first part the post-system, parties tend to favour the majority community.[18]

V. Perspective and Paradigm

The right to equality and Directives of State Policy of the Constitution did not create level playing field in securing equal opportunities to the Muslim since its enactments. The data available through national surveys by official agencies and expert committee reports suggest that while considerable progress has been achieved in some sectors, a large number of Muslims are still disadvantaged in terms of even accessing the basic necessities of life for survival with dignity. The Equal Opportunity Commission

Report. They are either discriminated or disproportionately denied of opportunities because of a variety of circumstances which are neither of their creation nor within their control to overcome.[19] The lapse may be of the institutional arrangements in place or the weakness of policies involved. The differential impact of some developmental policies are either not noticed or documented. It is this data and institutional deficit that the Equal Opportunity Commission Report addressed in an unmistakable terms. The object is removal of unfair discrimination and proactive creation of conditions in order to enable such neglected groups to avail of the constitutionally guaranteed right to equality. The new mechanism, therefore, should be such that, based on well-researched qualitative and quantitative data around the status of deprived groups, it should be able to influence policy (legislature), intervene in the implementation of laws and schemes (executive) and enable the accessing of equal justice under the law (judicial processes).

The development of such a mechanism and determining its structure, scope and functions by suggesting Anti Discrimination Law and Equal Opportunity legislations. The equalization of opportunity and Inclusive growth goes along within a sustainable pattern in the long run of empowerment of Muslims. The socialist and egalitarian model of the Indian Constitution envisaged a space for disadvantaged category of people and the complex nature of disabilities they have been suffering from. It is not easy to bring about equality of status and of opportunity for all through rule of law and democratic processes. Entrenched attitudes and conventional mindsets constitute a major limitation in bringing about social change. History is replete with instances of how well-intentioned initiatives have brought more misery than good when authoritarian methods were employed and balance of interests not maintained.

VI. Equalisation of Opportunity

In other words, social engineering through legal and democratic institutions and processes has to necessarily acknowledge group identities and opt for incremental and consensual change. The consensus model depends a great deal on evidence-based advocacy and a balance between liberty and freedom. With the market forces not being favourably disposed to ideals of equity and equality, it becomes the duty of the State to be proactive in the matter of equalization of opportunities for disadvantaged people. The human rights jurisprudence as it developed globally during the last few decades has decidedly supported State intervention against discriminatory practices even against private enterprise. Indian Constitutional law as interpreted and developed by the Supreme Court has also shown a remarkable trend to invoke the human rights discipline in constructing the egalitarian social order through qualitative and quantitative criteria. Courts sought measurable indices evaluated statistically to determine beneficiaries of affirmative action. The proposed Commission can profitably build on this trend with its evidence based advocacy to promote equality of opportunity to deprived sections.

The equality jurisprudence contained in the Constitution, interpreted and developed by Parliament and Judiciary in India is rich and dynamic to serve the social justice vision of the Republic. The challenge is to translate it into appropriate policies and programmes without disturbing the democratic commitment to rule of law and harmonious relations among the different communities and groups. Multi-cultural societies all over the world have been experimenting with diverse institutional mechanisms to achieve the desired results with varying degrees of success. India too set up almost a dozen commissions at the national level to look after the special interests of disadvantaged sections of society. They are doing their best to focus the attention of the authorities on the problems of communities entrusted to their care. However, the issue of equal opportunity in different walks of life to disadvantaged groups has not received the attention it deserved for want of detailed quantitative and qualitative data, adequate legislative support and vigorous public advocacy.

The unorganized sector and the vast mass of self-employed persons do need the support of the State to be able to share the opportunities provided by economic development.[20] The identity of the deprived sections is not so much based on caste and religion but on their common plight of deprivation and consequent inability to access equality of opportunity. They are people with per capita consumption of less than Rs. 15 per day whose numbers, we understand, exceed 500 million people. They do not belong to any one caste or religion. They largely come from among the Scheduled Castes, Scheduled Tribes, disabled persons, minorities and even from some sections of the majority communities. Thanks to the Constitution-makers, these persons are not helpless before law and the Constitution. They are endowed with rights and entitlements in respect of education, employment, health and dignity. The problem is with respect to their inability to assert the rights and fight discrimination. Our legal system can help only those who can reach the court and prove the discrimination based on facts and figures. The proposed Equal Opportunity Commission is expected to assume the role of a public advocate for the deprived groups. The evidence it collects and the arguments it constructs on the basis of equality jurisprudence can deliver reliefs and remedies administratively and wherever required, through the courts and tribunals.

VII. Equal Opportunity Commission

No community or group should feel discriminated against. Nor should any group suffer denial of equal opportunity for want of capacity to marshal facts and advance arguments based on them. If there are gaps and inadequacies in policies or programmes, the proposed watchdog body should be able to intervene effectively and restore equality of opportunity in each and every sector of public life. A culture of equality and fraternity should be cultivated so as to permeate every section of society if the Preambular Promise of Justice, Social, Economic and Political, has to be redeemed. This is a task in which the Equal Opportunity Commission will take a lead role with a missionary zeal. The various other commissions now functioning can be partners in this mission.

Perhaps the equal opportunity situation would have been different had the Government set up the Equal Opportunity

Commission immediately after the enactment of the Constitution. Now it is up to Government not to delay the establishment of the Commission. There are expectations generated among deprived groups including minorities that the proposed Commission would not just be a recommendatory body but one which can remedy the discrimination and denial of equal opportunity of deprived groups through appropriate, expeditious action. The country cannot afford to disappoint them and still hope to be a nation committed to equality, fairness and dignity. With the economy looking up and all the political parties subscribing to the ideal of inclusive development, the time is opportune for a breakthrough in the conventional style of administration of the social justice agenda. It is hoped that the Government would find the Equal Opportunity Commission Bill attached to this report suitable to be enacted immediately so that the Commission may be in place well before the end of the year.

Institutions are as good as the people who come to manage them particularly in its infancy. Special care should be taken in the constitution of the first Commission which will determine its character, capacity and esteem among the stakeholders. The attached Bill has attempted to structure the procedure constituting the Commission with a view to attract the best available persons for the onerous and challenging responsibilities entrusted to the Commission. Let the Equal Opportunity Commission herald a new era of hope and empowerment to the many "deprived groups" to enjoy the fruits of freedom and development and to live a life of dignity equal to their fellow citizens.

VIII. Conclusion and Suggestions

A qualitative improvement in Muslim education is prerequisite to be preventing discrimination.[21] India has one of the largest Muslim populations in the world (102 million) constituting 12 per cent of the total population.[22] The 64.5 per cent of Indian Muslims stay in rural India while 35.5 per cent live in urban areas. Most of the Muslims populations live in rural areas in the higher concentration States, while the urban Muslim population is much higher in States which have a lower percentage of Muslims.[23] The status of Indian Muslims has a poor human development status because of widespread illiteracy, low income, irregular employment, high incidence of poverty.[24] There are wide socio-economic diversities which vary from State to State and region to region.

The National Sample Survey Organization (NSSO), a Central Government body, has confirmed that India's largest religious minority is the most backward community on the educational front. Muslims' ratio in higher education is lower than even Scheduled Tribes (STs), considered most backward. Attached to the Union Ministry of Statistics and Programme Implementation, NSSO, in its report titled "Education in India, 2007-08: Participation and Expenditure", says that of 100 Muslims in the education system, just 10 are enrolled in high school and above. Similar ratio for STs is 11, Scheduled Castes (SCs) 12 and Other Backward Classes (OBCs) 14.

The report also says that high education among urban Muslims is lower than their counterparts in rural areas. This despite the fact that urban areas have better educational facilities. According to the NSSO report published on May 19, just seven out of 100 urban Muslims in the education system were enrolled in high school or above as compared to 12 in rural areas. Christians lead all communities—religious and social—in pursuing education, followed by Sikhs and OBCs. The report is based on the household survey on participation and expenditure in education conducted in its 64th round. The field work of the nationwide survey was carried out during July 2007 to June 2008.

The survey covered a random sample of 4,45,960 persons, from 63,318 rural households and 37,263 urban households spread over 7,953 villages and 4,682 urban blocks, covering the entire geographical area of the country. The access and empowerment and equalization of opportunities can be achieved by the proportionate allocation of resources under the plan according to population of Muslims. Till date socio-economic profiling of Muslims is generally not done on the lines of Scheduled Castes, Scheduled Tribes and Other Backward Classes. The State discrimination on this count is ventilated by special constitution of committee such as Gopal Singh Report, Sachar Committee, Ranganath Mishra Committee, N.R. Madhva Menon Committee and Amitabh Kundu Committee. The constitution and reports of these committees generally documents the obvious issues in an innovative ways. This also feeds appeasement theory and triggers hostility among a minority Hindus in the majority community who themselves feel endangered by Muslims. On the other hand Muslim feels unnecessarily excited about documented portrayal of their plight and ultimately shocked by perpetual betrayal and deep frustrations. There is need to come out of this doctrinaire legacy and marshal argument in the vocabulary of equalization of opportunity zealously guarded by the Constitution, rule of law and democratic governance. The government should not shy from fair documentation of Muslim condition under Census of India in honest way and thrash for solution by equalization demystifying doling out methodology and concession than that of rights and freedom. This randomly can be achieved by the proportionate allocation of resources according to population of Muslims and their lethal implementation.

NOTES

1. Nasreen Fazalbhoy, Sociology of Muslims in India: A Review, *Economic and Political Weekly*, June 28, 1997.
2. Nomani, Md. Zafar Mahfooz, *Conceptualization and Contextualization of Social Exclusion under Equal Opportunity Commission Report: Reflections and Appraisal*, [Paper submitted to National Conference on Exclusionary Perspectives for Muslims and Marginalized Groups, Maulana Azad National Urdu University, MANUU, Feb. 2010]
3. Robinson, F. (1983): 'Islam and Muslim Society in South Asia', Contributions to Indian Sociology, ns. 18 (2), pp. 301-05, (1986): 'Islam and Muslim Society in South Asia: A Reply to Das and Minault', Contributions to Indian Sociology, 20, pp. 97-104.
4. Lindholm, C. (1986): 'Caste in Islam and the Problem of Deviant Systems: A Critique of Recent Theory', Contributions to *Indian Sociology*, Vol. 20 (1), p. 61-73.
5. Madan, T.N. (1976): Muslim Communities of South Asia, (Revised and

enlarged edition, 1995), Vikas Publishing House, New Delhi. (ed) (1992): *Religion in India*, Oxford University Press, Delhi.

6. Minault, G. (1984): 'Some Reflections on Islamic Revivalism *vs.* Assimilation among Muslims in India', Contributions to *Indian Sociology*, 18, pp. 301-05.
7. Evans, Martin, (1998): "Behind the Rhetoric: The Institutional Basis of Social Exclusion and Poverty", *IDS Bulletin*, 29(1): 4249.
8. Bhalla, Ajit and Frederic Layepyre, (1997): "Social Exclusion: Towards an Analytical and Operational Framework", *Development and Change*, 28(3): 413-33.
9. Silver, Hilary, (1994): "Social exclusion and social solidarity: Three paradigms", *International Labour Review*, 133(5-6): 537-78.
10. Shariff, Abusaleh (1995): Socio-economic and Demographic Differentials between Hindus and Muslims in India, *EPW*, November 18, 1995 and Razzack, Azra and Gumber, Anil, Differentials in Human Development: A Case Empowerment of Muslims in India. Paper presented at a seminar organised by the NCAER, in November 2000.
11. National Commission for Minorities (1998-1999): *Annual Report* (un-tabled), p. 27.
12. Shariff, Abusaleh (1999): *India Human Development Report. A Profile of Indian States in the 1990's*. New Delhi: Oxford University Press, p. 121.
13. Government of India, Ministry of Human Resource Development (1986): *National Policy on Education*. Government of India, Ministry of Human Resource Development (1986).
14. Sachar, Rajender, Report 2006—Prime Minister High Level Committee on Social, Economic and Educational Status of Muslim Community of India, pp. 365-380.
15. Basant Rakesh (2007): "Social, Economic and Educational Conditions of Indian Muslims", *Economic and Political Weekly*, March 700, pp. 828-832.
16. Shah, Ghanshyam (2007): "The condition of Muslims", *Economic and Political Weekly*, 2007, pp. 836-843.
17. Ansari, A. Iqbal (2006): *Political Representation of Muslims in India 1952-2004*, Manak Publication Pvt. Ltd., New Delhi, p. 63.
18. Shahabuddin, Syed (2006): Indian Muslims, Legitimate Aspiration and Quest for due Representation in Legislature, *Mainstream*, December 22-28, pp. 39-45.
19. Ministry of Minority Affairs, Government of India, *Equal Opportunity Commission: What, Why and How*, N.R. Madhava Menon Committee Report, xvi (2008).
20. *Ibid.*, p. xvii.
21. Gopal Singh Panel Report: Government Statement and Comments, *Lok Sabha*, 24th August, 1990.

22. Bose, Ashish (1997): *Population Profile of Religion in India*. Delhi: B.R. Publishing Corporation.
23. Massey, James (1998): *Studies in Educational and Socio-Economic Problems of the Minorities in India*. A Report of the National Commission for Minorities.
24. Shariff, Abusaleh (2000): 'Relative Economic and Social Deprivation in India.' Paper presented at an international seminar on 'Multi-dimensional definition of poverty in India and Latin America', held at the International Development Centre, Oxford University, Oxford, October 27-28, 2000.

10

The Holistic Vision on the Empowerment of Muslims in the Twelfth Plan

M. Shabbir

On the basis of numerous national surveys regarding the minorities in India, the Muslims have been found to be the most backward in almost all aspects of life, whether it be social, educational, economical or their poor representation in employment (Public Sector). The High Power Gopal Singh Minority Panel report on minorities submitted in 1983 has stated that in 46 districts surveyed in 12 major States, it was astonishingly found that the percentage of the enrolment of Muslims' children of the elementary level (Class I to VIII) was much lower than that of the Muslim population in those districts, except in Madhya Pradesh (M.P.) which had slightly better record. The situation in Uttar Pradesh was the worst in this respect, wherein 12 districts surveyed, the enrolment of Muslim children was only 8.4 per cent.

Educational Rights of the minorities were regarded more important and they are guaranteed under Article 30 of the Indian Constitution of India. It is not only the implementation aspect or administrative response which is to be blamed, there are many perennial factors responsible directly for the educational backwardness of Muslims.

The Muslims earlier usually failed to avail fully the facilities of education, as enshrined under the Constitution *vide* (Article 30 because of the perceived taboos and prejudices against modern education, apart from their poor economic condition. Even Sir Syed Ahmad Khan, the founder of Aligarh Muslim University and many other educationaists like him had felt the dire need to make the Muslims aware that unless they take up modern education they would be left behind in the race of equality along with in the economic and social spheres. The Indian Constitution guarantees equal rights to all, but unfortunately despite the clear cut constitutional mandate, the judicial pronouncement to the effect, Constituent Assembly's debates, safeguards to minorities including Muslims particularly, with respect to educational rights and their entitlement to 'establish' and 'administer' the educational institutions of their choice have not been implemented by the State mainly due to prejudice, bias and other ulterior considerations.

The sorriful plight of the Muslim minorities can easily be assessed on the basis of their poor representation, much against their population ratio in almost all walks of life whether it be politics, defence, civil, executive legislative, judicial services, education, public sectors, private sectors, police, multinational companies or organizations.

The recommendations of the Sachar Committee report drew the attention of the nation towards the deficits of the majority of Muslims in education, livelihood and access to public service. its conclusion was that the Muslim community exhibits deficits and deprivation practically in all aspects of development. It found worryingly low school enrolments poor and high dropouts, even more for boys than girls. The Committee had also identified poverty to be the major barrier to education amongst Muslims as young children are expected to support their family rather than to study. There is good quality schools of government in the Muslim populated areas and also no residential hostels and exclusive girls schools. The scant schools do exist are highly understaffed with poorly motivated and incompetent teachers. Most of the children are truants or dropouts from their schools just to employ themselves in factories, *dhabas*, restaurants, private sectors for paltry sum of wages. Moreover, there is a poor representation of Muslims in the employment market across the States. The policies of economic liberalization have further sounded the death knell of most traditional occupations of Muslims like hand and power looms, silk and sericulture, garment making, tailoring, leather and automobiles repair, etc. Home based industries like embroidery, zari and chicken work which provided Muslim women stile, but low incomes are also gasping for survival. Formal banks and private money lenders often evade from extending credits/loans to Muslims. Young Muslim men and women face acute discrimination in government recruitment and the private sector appointment of Muslims is even more discouraging. Further, as identified by the Sachar Committee that normally Muslim settlements are systematically deprived of access to infrastructure and public services like power, piped water supplies and sewerage. Most of the remote villages do not have either proper schools or health facilities. As a result, the maternal mortality rates, incidences of malnutrition, under weight children and anaemic mothers are comparatively higher among Muslims.

In the estimation of Sachar Committee, the Muslims are not only the victims of poverty, rather have accepted inequality and discrimination as their inevitable fate. Muslims also suffer from recurring insecurity, because of devastating episodes of mass communal violence and the prejudiced law enforcement agencies. Muslims are usually blamed for every terror attack normally on flimsy, false and fabricated evidences thus are becoming the victim of long incarcerations and brutalities therein.

Thus, having discussed the prevailing socio-economic and educational status of Muslims in India along with the reports of the national surveys, it can be concluded that education of Muslims should be taken as a matter of highest priority in order to ameliorate them from their pathetic state of life. We have to promote multi-lingual education as instrument of social inclusion, confront inequality in educational institutions/opportunities, encourage the development of curricula which represent all communities. We have to address arbitrariness in national recognition of minorities, and their existence should be a question of fact.

Political participation and representation in governance structure are extremely essential to achieve equality. The factor of Muslim discriminations amongst the different communities which is primarily responsible for their backwardness, has to be removed once for all. It becomes the obvious duty of the state to remove such discrimination in order to flourish. Better utilization of waqf properties, productive utilization of money available through charity like *Zakaat*, education, and health and more effective participation in democratic process would definitely help the community to improve their status. There must be a general consensus amongst the Muslims about the need to generate data to evaluate and address the issues of backwardness. Policies of affirmative action need to be tuned to take into account the 'deficits' faced by the Muslims in higher education. The state must fulfil its obligation to provide affordable high quality education through the formal education system. It is the constitutional obligation of the Government under Article 21-A to provide education to the masses. It is the constitutional obligation of the State not to make any discrimination to allocate funds to Madarsas and at the same time, the state must fulfil its constitutional obligation under Article 350-A (Facilities for instruction in mother tongue at primary stage) in view of the large number of children with Urdu as their mother tongue. Urdu should be taught as an elective subject till graduation. *Bidi* workers, tailors and mechanics to be provided social security and social safety nets. Capacity building and assistance programmes NAMBARD (Bank) have considerably to benefit Muslims and improve substantially their socio-economic status. Effective steps be taken to instil a sense of security and confidence amongst the Muslims. Steps be introduced to specially direct credit to Muslims, create awareness of numerous credit schemes ensuring transparency in reporting of informations.

Even if the share of Muslim bodies is low and they under-represented segments can be involved in decision making process. Backward Muslims should be treated as a separate class and reservation be provided for them like other backward classes. Muslim reservation must continue as long as their backwardness exists in terms of their educational, social, economic, employment, cultural and political status. Extra budget must be further sanctioned for improving the plight of Muslim community.

Specific Suggestions for Improving the Plightful Status of Muslims

The following suggestions for the improvement of the condition of minorities particularly Muslims to be incorporated in the plan referred herein above having duly cogitated, deliberated and presented at the meet on March 30, 2011:

1. That the word **"Minority"** must be defined by the Parliament while amending by way of an insertion into Article 29 of the Constitution of India to end conflicting decisions of the judicial branch of the State.
2. That **10 per cent reservation of Muslims** of India must also be ensured in the services under the Union of India and in all States irrespective of any impediment in the name of religion, caste, language, region or otherwise.
3. That Rights of Muslim to equal opportunities and equal access to all natural and national resources deviant to any prejudices, predilections or preposterous argument must be made available under the rigours of law of the land.
4. That the Muslims reservation proportionate to their population must be made in the Parliament and State Legislative bodies by incorporating Muslim Dominated Areas through fresh delimitation of constituencies.
5. That proportionate to the population the representation of the Muslims in the **armed forces** under the Union of India must also be ensured by suitably amending the existing law or bringing in a new legislation thereto in the Parliament or otherwise.
6. That proportionate to the population, the representation of the Muslims in the **Police Force** and para military forces under the various States must also be made available to curb the menace of communal riots, regional riots, linguistic riots and caste riots.
7. That establishment of more minority educational institutions in the country be encouraged, promoted and established.

8. That **Right not to be Poor, Right to be Consulted and Right of Participation in the "Inclusive Economic Growth Model" of Development** in every walk of life must also be ensured without any discrimination whatsoever.
9. That the concept of **"Unity with Diversity"** must be promoted instead of Unity in Diversity.
10. That in the 33 per cent reservation of women in legislative bodies, a separate reservation for Muslim women must also be made that seeks to provide better education, health, hygiene, housing and skills to the Muslim women.
11. That the working of existing *Madarsas* must not be disturbed and they should be allowed to continue in imparting religious education without any State interference or otherwise.
12. That leadership building among the Muslims must be made the part of affirmative action through a system of incentives, enterprises and to ensure diversity at the work places. To achieve the target, public and private sectors must come together.
13. That Local Bodies and *Panchayati Raj* Institutions must be utilized to reflect the inclusive growth and human development.
14. That ideological indoctrination against Muslims by private and public undertakings, entities, institutions and organizations must be made a criminal offence of non-bailable and cognizable character.
15. That the status of Muslim places of worship must be maintained as of 1947 status. Moreover, heritage buildings and historical monuments associated with the Muslims must also be preserved, protected and promoted by the Union and State Government in real terms at the ground level.

Participation and Monitoring

1. A congenial atmosphere should be created to encourage the Muslims to come forward and enjoy the fruits of

development. The Muslims should actively participate in such activities to create the atmosphere.

2. Specific responsibility should be fixed on state officials to implement the policies, programmes and schemes initiated by the government for the welfare of the Muslim introduced from time to time.
3. The officials given such responsibility should be held personally responsible if they fail to implement such schemes.
4. Concrete measures are required for monitoring. It cannot be left entirely upon the officials or the system which is not capable of yielding positive results due to one reason or the other.
5. The Muslims must be included in the monitoring mechanism and their view should be given due weightage.
6. Emphasis should be made on proper propagation of welfare schemes amongst the Muslims and their implementation rather than paper work.
7. The schemes for the upliftment of Muslims must be prepared keeping in mind their specific circumstances wherein they are living.
8. The schemes preferably should be stated in the field which suits them most in affirmative manner.
9. To identify such areas and implement the scheme the help from expert groups and N.G.O.s who have the experience of working at the ground level should be sought.

A direct communication bridge is the need of the time between the Muslim community and the state for the success of any welfare measure for the Muslim. Both state and educational institutions especially the institutions of higher education may undertake this responsibility by providing them training and involving them into activities (i.e., debate, group discussions, communication skills, etc.) to bring out their inherent talent to help the planners to evolve the schemes best suited to Muslims on the one hand and on the other hand to sensitize the Muslims about their rights and duties in correct perspective.

Literacy

1. Schools should be opened in appropriate numbers consisting a substantial Muslim population.
2. Such schools must be in or near the place, where the substantial population of Muslims is settled.
3. Separate schools for girls in rural areas consisting of substantial Muslim population, should be opened from the level of primary schools.
4. The private schools in such areas getting financial aid from the government should be asked to admit every eligible Muslim child to a certain percentage.
5. The schools must be equipped with incentive schemes (Fee exemption, health check-ups, nutrition, etc.) along with activities of interest (i.e., sports, N.S.S., N.C.C.).
6. Special classes in such schools at convenient time for literate adult Muslims arranged as they also bear other responsibility in the family.
7. Efforts should be made to ensure that such schools should develop a scientific approach.
8. The monitoring of such schools beside officials must also be given to a committee consisting of 3 to 5 Muslims preferably whose children are studying in those schools.
9. It should be ensured that the funds allocated for achieving the literacy target must be utilized properly. The funds for creating and developing infrastructural facilities should be separate.

Training

1. Training Centres should be opened in and around the Muslim localities.
2. These Centres should assist to develop the skills not only in their traditional areas, i.e., weaving, tailoring, carpentry

etc., but also other developing areas, i.e., training in preparing of consumable items which are often produced by small scale industries.

3. The training centres must be made accountable for achieving their target and should provide complete information about the people so trained to the government and the committees which may be constituted for the aforesaid purpose.
4. The organizations providing for such trainings at national and State level should also be mandated to provide every help to such training centres.

Health

1. In remote areas where Muslim population is concentrated more Primary Health Centres should be opened.
2. A lady doctor must be posted at such Centre to ensure the benefit for Muslim girls and women.
3. In urban areas there are complaints that the doctors often neglect their duties for other monetary gain or sometimes even show an attitude of biasness towards Muslims. These issues must be resolved by initiating strict disciplinary action and fixing personal liability in such centres.
4. A Committee is to be formed to keep watch that medicines meant for distribution through these hospitals and medical centres are being distributed properly.

Economic Independence

1. Loan should be made easily available not only to generate employment opportunities or entrepreneurship but also artisans to start and extend their own work/business.
2. All the State owned banks and financial institutions should be asked to fix and achieve the targets in this respect.
3. In case of failure to achieve the target, responsibility of the person concerned should be fixed and the reasons for grant of such loans should also be ascertained.

4. The loans should be provided at a lower interest rate.

Job Opportunities

1. Education must be result oriented (i.e., may be used in practice) and should not be linked with degrees alone.
2. The State should adopt the policy of reservation in jobs for Muslims on the basis of recommendations made by Rangnath Misra Commission and the model adopted by Andhra Pradesh and Kerala where Muslims are differentiated not as religion but as a class or group of persons.
3. Tax incentives may be provided to the corporate sector reserving a certain percentage for Muslims.

Financial Assistance in Education

1. Scholarship must be extended from primary level to higher education.
2. Such scholarship must be extended to each and every student at least up to intermediate level.
3. At higher education level, it should be provided to all the girl students and at least 65 per cent to 70 per cent to the male students.
4. The renewal or extension of scholarship must be made without any consideration to vacation period.
5. The scholarship must be there with only one condition for clearing the examinations (i.e., no fixation of attendance or percentage of marks).

11

Educational Initiatives to Transform Muslim Community

Parvaiz Talib

Backwardness of Muslims is well recorded. It is substantiated by common place observation as well as Government statistics and reports. Different facets of backwardness are also in the sphere of common knowledge now. There is consensus on remedial measures also. It is now well established that *education* is the core and long term solution to address various facets of backwardness comprehensively.

This chapter attempts to present a framework to understand the range of educational initiatives required to address backwardness of Muslims. The chapter rests on the premise that roots of transformation of Muslims or for that matter any community/ society lies in education only.

Muslims as a community are faced with two key challenges on educational front:

Education of the Elite: There is a concern of lack of excellence among Muslims. This is reflected both at national and global level. The representation of Muslims in elite jobs and institutions of excellence is dismal. The weight of a community is not decided by its teeming millions. Rather, it is because of a select few who have made a mark life through their professional accomplishment. It is said that minority rules the world. We can cite the example of Jews as a community. Though numerically insignificant, they control the levers of society on various accounts. Muslims unfortunately do not carry such weight. There is a need for creating a spirit of excellence among Muslims. Therefore, the focus of these efforts needs to be on *quality*. Efforts need to aim at producing future leaders from amongst Muslims in varied walks of life.

Education of the Masses: Vast majority of Muslims are leading life at the periphery. The benefits of mainstreams education are either not available to them or they, themselves, have decided to remain away from them (for numerous reason). These teeming millions are at the bottom rung of the society and are leading precarious existence. They face the brunt of any social or economic upheaval. There is a pressing need of initiating efforts for providing vocational and technical education for such a group. They need to be equipped with useful skills that can help them earn a reasonable living.

This chapter presents a framework which may be useful in crystallizing interventions at both the fronts, i.e., quality as also quantity. This chapter draws heavily from two successful models that have been worked out and could be instructive to draw lessons from. I leverage my experience from an administration assignment also as Director of Coaching and Guidance Centre of AMU.

Let us first understand the nature of challenge on first account, i.e., inculcating a spirit of excellence among Muslims. There is a genuine concern of lack of representation of Muslims in elite governmental jobs and institutions. The success rate in the following competitive examination is a good indicator of spirit of excellence in a community:

- National Talent Search Examination;
- National Defence Academy;
- IIT/AIPMT;
- CAT; and
- Elite governmental jobs (Civil Services, Judicial Services, Specialized Services like Engineering Services, Economic Services, Statistical Services, etc.).

The representation of Muslims among these competitive examinations is far from satisfactory.

There is a need to initiate measures to increase representation of Muslims in these examinations. There have been attempts to improve success rate of Muslims among Civil Services—the most prestigious examination out of the lot mentioned above. Hamdard Study Circle, New Delhi has been a notable endeavour in this regard. AMU's Coaching and Guidance Centre initiated a programme to improve success rate of students studying in AMU schools in NTSE. The programme did make an impact in creating a competitive spirit among students at a young age. There is need to broaden and deepen these efforts by identifying pockets wherein these efforts can be initiated. However, the key issue is sustaining these efforts over a sufficiently long period so that meaningful results could be obtained.

The interventions identified above, though important, suffer from a major handicap. It presumes that there is a class of students who have basic potential to clear these prestigious examinations. This basic premise is often not true. In the first place, a class of such students is not available in substantial number that could provide a broad enough base for these efforts. For example, the percentage of graduates among Muslims is lower than rest. Then, students who aspire for these examinations operate with a number of handicaps. Many of them have a basic deficiency in language and comprehension. They suffer from dwindling motivation level also. The sustained effort is often missing. Effective counselling help is also not available. Therefore, majority of them end up wasting prime period of their life in an option for which they had no ability or aptitude in the first place. Moreover, the intensity of competition in these examinations is becoming tougher day by day. Therefore, the success rate continues to be a cause of concern with no appreciable improvement, despite efforts initiated by some well meaning persons.

Therefore, there is a need of second level strategy, i.e., creating a spirit of excellence and imbibing a competitive spirit among students at a young age. Moulding of young minds to assume a lead role in society begins at the primary level. This aim can be achieved by establishing a school with a difference. The author had observed the emergence of such a school from close quarter. Established under the aegis of Eklavya Educational Foundation (*www.eklavya.org*) in 1996, this school has the following features:

- It is based on Maria Montessaric method of education, wherein personal attention is given to each student to ensure blossoming of young minds as per their natural inclination. Therefore, batch size is restricted to 16 students per batch in the early classes. The batch strength is increased gradually, but even at highest level, i.e., class XII, the prescribed batch strength is 35 only. The school is designed to serve a maximum of 1,400 students only.
- The school requires an investment of 15 crore.
- The school has a gestation period of 15 years. Only after this threshold period, meaningful results start emerging.

Creating such a school shall lay the foundation of creating a spirit of excellence among Muslims on a sustained basis. Once this model is successfully crystallized, it can be replicated to create a chain of such institutions. The focus of these institutions shall be nurturing young minds from the primary school. It is a common experience that students who undergo schooling with a sound base are able to withstand the rigours of higher education on their own and are self dependent. They are, therefore, not too heavily dependent on coaching for competing in prestigious examinations. Even, if some coaching input is required, its role is only supplementary in nature.

The products of such a school are exposed to a range of role models during this schooling period. They are then exported to carve out a path best suited to them, on their own. However, the spirit of excellence imbibed in them remains their hallmark, irrespective of their chosen field of endeavour. They are groomed to be thought leaders who become change agents in their respective fields.

Education of the Masses

As noted earlier, a substantial section of Muslim population in India is leading a life at the periphery. The target group falling in this category comprises those who are *illiterates,* i.e., they have never had access to educational opportunity, *dropouts* i.e. those who did enroll themselves in a school but could not continue their education because of multitudes of factors. Then, there is significant chunk of students who are either studying or have passed out Madarsas—the Islamic Seminaries.

There is urgent need to initiate to measures so that this group is able to acquire such skills which helps them earn a reasonable living. It is said that poverty anywhere is threat to prosperity everywhere. There is pressing need to bring this group in the economic mainstream.

The author had an occasion to study and experience a model being initiated and crystallized in southern India. This movement, called the community colleges, is being run under the stewardship of a Jesuit Priest Dr. Xavier Alphonse. Launched in 1995, with first Community College, the spread has increased manifold, with more than 200 community colleges across India—though majority of them are still located in Tamil Nadu. (www.IRDCE.com) These Community Colleges (CCs) have two simple motto, namely; *include the excluded* and the pass-outs of CCs ought to be *fit for life and fit for job.* The second aspect distinguishes CCs from Vocational Coleges. The curriculum of CCs is designed to ensure the following proportion:

Work skills	40 per cent
Life skills	40 per cent
Preparations for employment	20 per cent

In *work skills,* the organization spearheading this movement, i.e., Indian Centre for Research and Development in Community Education (ICRDCE), has crystallized as many as 50 traits/skills for which training can be imparted. However, each community college is exhorted to undertake *need analysis* of the area where CC is located to ascertain the skill in demand. Accordingly, they are advised to launch the courses in line with the requirement of the market.

The component of *life skills* is common to all courses. This includes knowledge of basic functional English, computer skills and life coping skills, e.g., how to set goals in life, maintaining a positive attitude, stress management and the like. The detailed work books for work skills as also life skills have been prepared by this organization with step by step lesson plans. A particular CC needs to just pick up the work book and deliver the contents efficiently as per the specified plan.

The component comprising *preparation for employment* includes industrial training and, later, basic training on how to face interviews, etc. This prepares students to face the employment market confidently.

The experience of these CCs suggests that 75 per cent of pass-outs are able to get a job after these, one year, courses. The range of emoluments is between Rs. 2,000 to 9,000, to begin with. The remaining ones either opt for self-employment, while some of them get inspired to pursue higher education. For this group ICRDCE has worked out a system of credit transfer with their affiliating agency, i.e., Tamil Nadu Open University. The pass-outs of CCs get admission into courses like B.Sc. (IT), BBA or B.Com., etc., depending on students' interest. The system has benefited approximately 80,000 students till date.

A typical CC is expected to offer training in 4 chosen skills. The ICRDCE advises the CCs to keep their investment in infra-structure low. One such CC is expected to incur a sum of Rs. 5 lakh per annum as operating expenses. Sixty per cent of that sum is recovered through fee from students the remaining amount needs to be arranged by management of the CC through donations or some other innovative scheme like opening a sales counter for the output of the skill for which the training is imparted.

There is a need for spread of this model which has been so successfully implemented in Southern India. It is expected that these initiatives can meaningfully address problem of huge of mass of Muslims and other disadvantaged sections, comprehensively. We shall then be able to use our key national resource, i.e., human resource to our advantage. They shall become our assets rather liability.

The efforts on both the fronts highlighted above shall be supervised and guided by a Research and integration council. This council shall work to deepen and broaden the initiatives on both the fronts. The Council shall act as a think tank and shall carry out relevant researches to become a resource base for any such initiative. They shall study efficiency of alternate forms of governance and suggest best form for NGOs—that shall spearhead these initiatives. They shall also undertake researches on emerging traits and skills for particular geographic areas. That shall also become a coordinating agency among various NGOs and shall ensure information dissemination of best practices. Moreover, this council shall create live models on both these accounts that can be replicated across the length and breadth of the country.

12

Educational Empowerment of Minorities in Twelfth Five Year Plan

Abdul Waheed

As a prelude to the proposal it seems appropriate to mention briefly the initiatives which the Government of India has taken so far for educational empowerment of minorities, mainly Muslims. The Government did not take note of "minorities" prior to setting up High Level Committee by Ministry of Home Affairs in May 1980.

1. The "Initiatives" for the welfare of "minorities" began with the announcement of Prime Minister's 15-Point Programme in 1983.
2. Maulana Azad Education Foundation was established in 1989 as a voluntary organization, registered under Societies Registration Act, to formulate and implement educational schemes and plans for the benefit of the educationally backward minority in particular and weaker sections in general and to provide grants-in-aid to voluntary organizations. The Foundation carry out its objectives out of the interest accrued on the investment of the corpus fund which was Rs. 550 crore as on 31.8.2010.
3. Recognition of "some minority groups as educationally backward" and promise to pay greater attention for their educational development in National Policy on Education (1986). Subsequently, Programme of Action (POA) was formulated in 1992 which spelt out measures for the

educational development of minorities. Some of the major initiatives conceived were as follows:

(a) Setting up Early Childhood Education Centres in schools imparting traditional education and in minority concentration areas.
(b) Introduction of secular education in institutions of traditional education.
(c) Under Area Approach special attention will be paid to create schools in 40 minority concentration districts for promoting access of minorities school education.
(d) Vocational and Technical education was conceived to be promoted by measures such as opening community polytechnics, utilising 15 per cent time of curriculum for training in local crafts/trades and to arrange evening classes for children of artisans/agricultural labourers at primary school level, introduction of vocational courses in higher secondary schools specially catering to educationally backward minorities, ensuring benefits of technical education programmes to minority educational institutions, and setting up Crafts Training Institutes in identified minority artisan concentration blocks, with 80 per cent seats for artisans' children.
(e) Establishment of State Resource Centres in 4 Universities namely Aligarh Muslim University, Osmania, Jamia Millia and Marathwada Universities with the grant of Rs. 65 lakh for providing coaching to minority students for various competitive examinations.

Besides, there were measures related with minority languages and training/orientation programmes for principals and teachers of minority institutions. All measures related with minority languages such as compilation of statistics, preparation of text-books, appointments of teachers, etc., were assigned to States for implementation.

4. Area Intensive and Madarsa Modernisation schemes were launched during Eighth Five Year Plan (1992-1997) in

1993. These two schemes were merged together into one in Tenth Five Year Plan (1997-2002). While Area Intensive Scheme (AIS) was launched to promote modern education, Madarsa Modernisation aimed at introducing modern subjects in institutions of traditional education. Under AIS 100 per cent financial assistance was provided to the State Governments and the voluntary organizations for the following programmes:

(i) Establishment of new primary/upper primary schools, non-formal education centres.
(ii) Strengthening of educational infrastructure and physical facilities in the Primary/Upper Primary Schools.
(iii) Opening of multi-stream residential higher secondary schools for girls to impart studies in Science, Commerce, Humanities and Vocational Courses.

Tehsil/Block was the unit for the administration of this scheme. Ministry of Welfare, on the basis of 1981 Census data, identified 325 Tehsils/Blocks of 89 districts spread over 13 States and 3 Union Territories for the implementation of the scheme.

5. Hence during three Five Year Plans, i.e., Eighth, Ninth and Tenth, the only substantive scheme was AIS and Madarsa Modernisation. Before making Sachar Committee Report public, 'Revised Prime Minister's 15-Point Programme was announced in June 2006. The Programme was classified into four categories, i.e., (a) Enhancing Opportunities for Education, (b) Equitable Share in Economic Activities and Employment, (c) Improving the Conditions of Living of Minorities, and (d) Prevention and Control of Communal Riots. The category (a) of the programme prescribes 6 measures which are as follows:

(i) Equitable availability of Integrated Child Development Services (ICDS): Under the scheme services will be provided through Anganwadi Centres for holistic development of children and for the health of pregnant women. These services will include supplementary nutrition, immunization, health check-up, referral services, pre-school and non-formal education. A certain percentage of ICDS projects and Anganwadi Centres will be located in minority concentrated villages.

(ii) Under the Sarva Shiksha Abhiyan, the Kasturba Gandhi Balika Vidyalaya Scheme, and other similar Government schemes, it will be ensured that a certain percentage of such schools are located in villages/ localities having a substantial population of minority communities for improving their access to school education.

(iii) Central assistance will be provided for recruitment and posting of Urdu language teachers in primary and upper primary schools that serve population in which at least one-fourth belong to that language group.

(iv) Area Intensive and Madarsa Modernization Programmes will substantially be strengthened and implemented effectively.

(v) Schemes for pre-Matric and post-Matric scholarships for students from minority communities will be formulated and implemented.

(vi) A certain proportion of new ITIs will be located in minority concentrated areas in order to upgrade the technical skills of people from minority communities.

6 As a sequel to Revised Prime Ministers' 15-Point Programme, findings and recommendations of Sachar Committee and Prime Minister's announcement that 15 per cent grant in every scheme may be earmarked for minority's development, some schemes, i.e., Pre-Matric, post-Matric, merit-cum-means scholarships; schemes for coaching and multi-sectoral district development programme in 90 identified minority concentration districts were started during Eleventh Plan Period under Ministry of Minority Affairs.

7. Except the programme of Madarsa Modernization,

> establishment of Urdu Academies in three Universities and a nominal grant to AMU for its two upcoming campuses in Murshidabad and Mallappuram, no initiatives of Ministry of Human Resource Development can be said exclusive for Muslims during the Eleventh Five Year Plan. The Ministry did not mention AIS in its steps taken for the educational development of minorities in Eleventh Plan. All the steps, which the Ministry claim for educational development of minorities, are the part and parcel of schemes whose benefits are available either to all citizens of the country or to minorities, SCs, STs, equally. Allocating a proportion of schools, KGBVs, Jan Siksha Sansthan, and Model Degree Colleges, proposed to be established during the Eleventh Five Year Plan, in minority concentration districts (MCDs) does not ensure its benefits to minorities.

It is evident that most of the initiatives like opening of Primary/ Upper Primary schools, Early Childhood Care Centres, etc., in minority concentration areas are integral part of policies and programmes launched for people of India. Their benefit should legally be flown to each and every individuals irrespective of his/her social and religious affiliation.

Many other initiatives like training of Principals and Teachers of minority educational institutions, programme for coaching, academies for Urdu, etc., are insubstantial in nature and may be referred as "tokenism" for minorities mainly Muslims. Very few initiatives like Area Intensive, Madarsa Modernization, Maulana Azad Education Foundation, and Scholarships can be said somehow substantial in nature. Multi-sectoral District Development Programme, the flagship scheme of Government of India cannot principally be called for the development of minorities but the development of the district in which 25 per cent or more population is of minorities. Since the implementation of these schemes is not legally binding, their implementation has remained highly ineffective.

Thus these initiatives can be said lacking social justice, the cardinal principle of Indian Constitution referring to "equality only among equals. To treat unequals as equals is to perpetuate inequality. The humanness of society is determined by the degree of protection it provides to its weaker, handicapped and less gifted members", says Justice Rangnath Mishra in his report on Religious and Linguistic Minorities. Hence, logically it implies that the higher is the marginality of a group, the greater should be affirmative action for it. Nevertheless, this principle has so far not been applied in the case of Muslims who have been declared by Ministry of HRD, Government of India as "national educationally backward minority" in 1993 and lagged far behind than even Scheduled Castes and Scheduled Tribes on various indicators of human development.

Proposals

It is, therefore, following proposals must be taken into consideration for the educational empowerment of minorities in Twelfth Five Year Plan:

1. The principle of social justice must be invoked for the preparation of exclusive schemes for Muslims as they are highly deprived groups among minorities and other weaker sections of the society like SCs and STs.
2. Unit of administration for such schemes must primarily be locality or habitation, like Ambedkar Village Scheme for SCs, in which 25 per cent and above population is of Muslims. Block or tehsil or district as a unit for administering minority welfare schemes does not ensure the flow of benefits to Muslims.
3. Multi-sectoral District Development Programme should be transformed into uni-sectoral (Education) development programme and its benefits be extended to all minority concentration habitation.
4. Implementation of schemes must legally be binding on implementing agencies.

5. If any scheme is not implemented during plan period unutilized grant either must be carried forward in the next plan or it may be transferred to the corpus fund of Maulana Azad Education Foundation whose grants-in-aid should be available to minorities in ratio of their population.
6. A separate budgetary sub-plan must be created for the development of Muslims in the way that governments have done for SCs and STs.
7. *School Education*: POA 1992, recommendation of Prime Minister's High Level Committee and Revised Prime Minister's 15-Point Programme underscore the need of school education to minorities and, therefore, sharper focus must be given to promote access of Muslims to qualify school education. The goal may be achieved through following measures:
   (a) Apart from creation of Primary and Upper Primary schools under SSA or as per Right to Education Act 2009, co-educational non-residential Senior Secondary School of quality education must be created in every rural-urban habitation of Muslim concentration.
   (b) Centrally funded and managed Residential Senior Secondary School for boys, like Jawahar Navodya Vidyalaya, must be created in every minority concentration Block.
   (c) One of the major objectives of Area Intensive Scheme was to open multi-stream residential Higher Secondary School for girls. The objective has not so far been achieved. Therefore, such schools for girls must be created in every minority concentration Block.
   (d) The Ministry of HRD claim that "continued efforts have been made to increase enrolment of Muslim girls in KGBVs" which have been created under SSA in educationally backward Blocks for imparting only primary education (i.e., from class VI to class VIII) to out of school and dropout girls of Scheduled Castes/Scheduled Tribes,

OBCs, minority's and general population below poverty line. However, empirical evidences show that many KGBVs deny admission to Muslim girls on the pretext that the share of minorities in admission is only 25 per cent. Hence, it seems warranted that the share of minorities in these schools must be according to the proportion of their population in the Block.

(e) Corpus fund of Maulana Azad Education Foundation may substantially be increased to at least rupees five thousand crore in Twelfth Five Year Plan and its grants-in-aid may be allocated to minorities in proportion to their population in order to promote voluntary efforts in the creation of schools.

(f) Reservation in admission to minorities in Jawahar Navodya Vidyalayas, like that of Scheduled Castes and Scheduled Tribes, may be given in proportion of their population in the district.

8. *Vocational Education*: Sharper focus should also be given to promote access of minorities to vocational education. This is highly critical for Muslims as it may promote modernization of traditional craft and employment among them. Although the Government has shown its commitment in this regard through various policy instrument, the goal has so far not been achieved. The following steps may prove catalyst for promoting vocational education among minorities mainly Muslims:

(a) Schools, which may be called Learning-Earning schools, may be opened in Muslim artisans concentration localities. These schools would certainly attract children of poor families which, instead of enroling their children in schools, prefer to send them for either earning or learning some craft.

(b) Grant to Madarsas for opening mini ITIs may substantially be enhanced.

(c) Every Muslim managed institutions of higher, professional and technical education must be enjoined to open vocational courses and the requisite grants may be provided to them.

(d) Reservation of minorities in admission to Government ITIs should be made as per the proportion of their population in the district.

(e) As per the recommendation of Prime Minister's High Level Committee pre-entry qualification for admission to ITIs for Muslims should be reduced from Matriculation to Class VIII. Further, the eligibility for admission to ITIs should also be extended to Madarsa educated children. Ministry of Minority Affairs' merit-cum-means scholarship should be provided to all minority children, receiving vocational education either from public or private institutions.

(f) A polytechnic should be established in each minority concentration block.

9. *Higher and Technical Education*: Providing greater access and equal access to higher and technical education are the goals of Education Policy of India 1986 and of Eleventh Five Year Plan (2007-12). Muslims deserve much attention of this policy as their gross enrolment rate in higher education is less than half of the national average. Following steps are desirable for enhancing participation of Muslims in higher and technical education:

(a) Like Scheduled Castes/Scheduled Tribes, eligibility criteria for admission to higher and technical education should be relaxed for Muslims as a large number of them cannot compete with non-Muslim students.

(b) Eighty eight colleges of higher education were proposed to open in minority concentration districts during Eleventh Five Year Plan. These colleges must necessarily be of Science and Commerce and located near Muslim concentration towns.

(c) All minority students of technical and professional education should be provided merit-cum-means scholarship irrespective of their institutions, private or public.

(d) Like Baba Saheb Bhimrao Ambedkar Central university in Lucknow, in which 50 per cent admission are reserved for SCs/STs, university should be created for minorities.

10. *Promotion of Urdu*: We need nothing more than what is laid down in POA 1992, and Revised Prime Minister's 15-Point Programme as well as recommendations of Prime Minister's High Level Committee for the promotion of Urdu. All the three policy instruments explicitly mention that facility of Urdu teaching is to be provided in all schools, having 25 per cent Urdu speaking students. However, it has not been implemented so far. Discrimination against Urdu is both overt and covert. For example Guidelines of SSA and Right to Education Act in regard to Urdu mention that facilities of Urdu teaching will be provided on demand. As this condition gives ample scope to bureaucrats for discriminating against Urdu, we propose that the condition must immediately be removed and Urdu teaching should be made mandatory. Besides, following recommendation of Prime Minister's High Level Committee should also immediately be implemented

    (a) Often Urdu schools have teachers who have no knowledge of Urdu. This problem is partly compounded by the fact that posts of Urdu teachers are reserved for the SCs/STs and such candidates are not available. This anomaly needs to be corrected urgently.

    (b) High quality Urdu medium schools should be opened in areas wherever there is demand for them.

    (c) Urdu should be introduced as an optional subject in all government and government-aided schools.

13

Muslims of Govandi, Mumbai: A Micro Level Study of their Socio-Economic Conditions

Abdul Haleem Kidwai

A Brief Historical Overview

Although the Muslims arrived at western coast of India as early as the seventh century, it was with the advent of the Allaudin Khilji in the late thirteenth century that the political presence was established in the Deccan region. This was further consolidated by Muhammad bin Tughlaq's decision to transfer his capital from Delhi to Daulatabad. During the medieval period, there was considerable tussle for supremacy in the Marathi region of the Deccan. It was the battle ground for the Bahmani Sultanates and its factions (Adil Shahis and Nizam Shahis), the Mughals and the Marathas and the Marathas emerged victorious. However, their dominance did not last long because the Marathas were defeated by the British and by early nineteenth century, it became a part of the British Empire and came to be known as the Bombay Presidency and Province.

Throughout the British period, Muslims in Bombay had been under-represented[1] in the public services and in the education sector. As Christine Dobbin notes, "By the mid-nineteenth century, the Muslim community throughout the Presidency was noted for its unwillingness to espouse the new English education. The problem was particularly acute in the cities, where Muslims in general spoke Urdu and so required a separate system of elementary schools before they could go even to the Anglo-Vernacular level."[2]

The present day state of Maharashtra came into existence in 1956 after the State Reorganization Commission was formed and the Marathwada region, which was originally part of the Nizam-ruled state of Hyderabad, was included in Maharashtra. Muslims constitute 10.6 per cent of the population of Maharashtra and the distribution of it follows the national trend, that is, they have a higher share in the urban population. They are 17.5 per cent of the urban population of Maharashtra but only 5.5 per cent of the rural population[3].

Unfortunately, Maharashtra also follows another national trend, that is, high incidence of urban poverty. 55 per cent of the urban Muslim population of Maharashtra is below poverty line while the figure for rural poverty is lower which stands at 28 per cent[4]. This makes the study of urban poverty among Muslims in general and among Muslims of Maharashtra particularly important.

The Need for Micro-level Studies

Although the Sachar Committee report has gathered a large body of data on the condition of Muslims in urban areas and it is established that they are the poorest community[5] in urban areas, there has been little research on the *processes* responsible for their poverty. As Steve Wilkinson writes, "I argue that these (data in Sachar report) tell us far less than we might wish about the processes of discrimination and the major factors that may be responsible for Muslim disadvantage, which prevents us from designing the best government and NGO interventions to deal with problems of minority community faces."[6]

However, it is important to note that it is difficult with the available macro-level data to find out the underlying causes of poverty among Muslims in India. Therefore, in order to answer the question of **why** Muslims are poor, there is a need to gather data at the micro-level which will look at both the quantitative and qualitative aspects of poverty among Muslims. As Abu Saleh Shariff argues, "There is a need to undertake focused micro-studies to clearly understand the nature, type and magnitude of socio-economic problems faced by various communities in rural and urban India."[7]

This chapter is an attempt to address this lacuna in the literature on poverty among Muslims by carrying out a micro-level study in Govandi, Mumbai which was then supplemented with fieldwork in Mumbra, Thane.

Govandi and Mumbra : A Sketch[8]

Govandi is one of the poorest areas of Mumbai and has a high concentration of Muslim population residing there. A sizeable section (41.3 per cent) of Govandi's population lives below the poverty line and over four-fifth (81.4 per cent) of the population lacks adequate housing and lives in slums/chawls. Govandi has a number of localities within it, the prominent ones being Rafiq Nagar, Tata Nagar, Lallubhai Compound, Gautam Nagar, Sanjay Nagar, Shivaji Nagar, Baiganwadi and Lotus Colony. Although the majority of the residents of Govandi share a common religious background, they come from a number of different States—Andhra Pradesh, Bihar, Gujarat, Karnataka, Maharashtra, Tamil Nadu, Uttar Pradesh among others. Of which the majority are from Uttar Pradesh (50.6 per cent) followed by Maharashtra (25 per cent) and Bihar (9.7 per cent).

Mumbra comprises of 19 wards and came under Thane Municipal Corporation in 1986. It is about 30 kilometres away from Govandi. It too, like Govandi, is a Muslim majority area and has a population of around 8 lakh.[9]

Although both these areas are marked by socio-economic deprivation (as will become evident from the next section), in the public imagination these are conceived as criminal areas. In the public discourse the marginalization faced by the residents of these localities is pushed into the background. If one searches for Govandi or Mumbra in the websites of leading newspapers[10], the results are reports of theft, robbery, murder and other crimes whereas the poor socio-economic status of these localities remains underreported. Consequently, the attention of the public as well as the policy-makers shifts from tackling the multiple disadvantages faced by the community to restoring 'law and order'. Therefore, the appropriate course of action is not to open more police stations but schools and hospitals, this will facilitate the inclusion of the community in the 'mainstream'.

Findings from Govandi and Mumbra

In this section, the author discusses the condition of the Muslims of Govandi in the light of the data he had collected from 100 households[11] with the help of the household questionnaire. The author has also included his observations as well as verbatim quotations of the respondents (mostly of those who had given indepth interviews).

Before proceeding further, it would be appropriate to present a brief profile of the respondents. A total of 100 households were taken. 51 of these were from Uttar Pradesh while the remaining 49 were from Bihar. The total population of these households was 600 residents of which 321 were from Uttar Pradesh and 279 were from Bihar. The selected group was of Muslim households which had migrated either from Uttar Pradesh or Bihar and were residents of either of the two localities of Govandi, namely, Rafi Nagar and Tata Nagar.

There were two main reasons for choosing migrants from these two States. The first was that these households are not only a religious minority but also a linguistic minority which in turn creates the potential from them to be doubly excluded—on the basis of religion as well as language. The second was that the author was fluent in both Hindi and Urdu which are the mother-tongues of these migrants, thus, making it easier to communicate and build rapport with the respondents.

The population under study was mostly young. Only 6.7 per cent of the total population was above 60 years of age while 25 per cent of the population were children, that is, between the age group of 0 to 14 years. Thus, the significant share of the population was in the working age group, that is, between the age of 15 to 60 years.

The author has divided the following section in two parts. The first deals with the living conditions of the Muslims in Govandi while the second section deals with their socio-economic status. In the living conditions section—housing, health, water, sewage and garbage disposal—are discussed. On the other hand, the socio-economic section looks at the employment status, education levels, access to credit and asset ownership.

Living Conditions of Govandi (and Mumbra) Muslims

Housing

Govandi is mostly a slum area and lacks adequate facilities. Amita Baviskar has defined a slum as "any area which has a very congested settlement and a place that, because there are not adequate services, in the sense of wide roads or the provision of electricity, water, etc., and the houses are in a dilapidated condition, might actually be a hazard to the health or the safety of the people who live there."[12]

In Govandi, there are a few pockets of non-slum areas as well which have buildings. However, most of these buildings are poorly maintained. In the sample covered for this study, 86 per cent of the households were living in slums or *chawls*. Even those residing in flats did not have spacious or luxurious flats. Most of these flats were small and cramped.

Since the houses were small, the room density in these areas was particularly high. 69 per cent of the households had a room density ranging from 4 to 6 persons per room. Apart from the obvious issues of lack of privacy, discomfort caused by these cramped conditions, there were certain hazards as well. For example, in a number of houses of the slum, there was one room which was partitioned off by a curtain or a thin wooden plank with the living/ sleeping area on the one side and the kitchen on the other. Proper ventilation was missing in many cases which exposed the household members to smoke and heat. This was particularly dangerous for the toddlers and young children living in the house because they would play and move about near the kitchen rendering them vulnerable to getting burnt. Another issue that came forth was that such an environment was not conducive to studying at all. One student remarked "*My family does want me to study and so do I but it is simply not possible in my home. You can see yourself. There are 7 people living here (referring to his two room house) and someone or the other wants to watch TV or chit-chat. There is too much noise and distraction here. If the government cannot give us good homes it should at least provide for libraries or reading rooms for us*". Another health hazard was the fact that these houses provided little or no protection from mosquitoes leaving the residents prone to malaria, dengue and other diseases.

However, the most deplorable aspect of poor housing conditions is the lack of toilets and bathrooms within the house. The people have to rely on community toilets and bathrooms. A number of the households (29%) do not have a separate bathroom but the problem is more severe with regard to toilets within the house (67% of the households do not have a toilet). This is not only a source of inconvenience, it poses more serious problems. The first is the issue of lack of proper hygiene and the health risks it poses (I had visited some of the public toilets/bathrooms of Govandi and they were filthy). The second issue is a more fundamental one and it is of human dignity. People should not be compelled into using public toilets/bathrooms. As one of the respondents said "*At times it is so humiliating to queue up to go to the toilet... I am saving up money to move into a flat and this (going to public toilets) would be one of the important reasons for doing so. There is no 'izzat' (dignity) living like this.*"

As it becomes evident from the above discussion, the housing conditions of Govandi are abysmal. However, on a positive note, high rates of ownership were reported. 64 per cent of the households owned their own house. Nonetheless, it is important to recall that not all these slums have been regularized (only those who have established that they were in Mumbai before 1995 have been formalized) and, therefore, are 'illegal' and subject to removal at any time by the authorities. The 'illegal' status of some of these areas gives an excuse to the authorities not to provide essential services to the residents.

The housing condition in Mumbra (of those covered in the sample) was significantly better than the residents of Govandi[13], in view of the fact that, a large number of the respondents were living in flats and not in slums/*chawls*. Some of them were living in *chawls*, however, every household that the author covered had both a bathroom and toilet inside. The main reason for better housing condition in Mumbra was the availability of low-cost housing in Mumbra. Most of the respondents had migrated from Mumbai (including from Govandi) after selling their property in Mumbai (which in most cases was a house in a slum/*chawl*). The money obtained from selling their property in Mumbai was enough to buy a flat in Mumbra. Some respondents also informed that they were left with enough money to expand their business even after purchasing a flat. However, a large number of residential buildings in Mumbra are 'unauthorized' that is they have not been approved by the Thane Municipal Corporation (TMC). Hence, the tag of 'illegality' remains with a section of the population of both Govandi and Mumbra.

One important finding that emerged during the study was that the residents of both Govandi and Mumbra argued that they felt safe in these areas and that is one of the main reasons for them staying there. In fact, even those respondents who could afford to move out of these areas said that they were unwilling to do so. They claimed that living with Muslims ensures the safety of life and limb which is not possible when living in a non-Muslim locality. A respondent from Govandi said "*We are doubly oppressed because we are poor and we are Muslims. Being poor means that the government doesn't care about us and being Muslim means that society thinks of us as outsiders. It is not uncommon to be labelled Pakistani or anti-Indian. At least living here* (in Govandi) *means that the community is with you. If I were to live somewhere else, who would be there to help me? Here, we have our own people who are always willing to assist us*". A resident of Mumbra echoed the same sentiment "*Living together gives us the chance to come together as a community and try to make improvements*".

However, there is a darker side to this idea of 'living with the community'. It should not be perceived simplistically as a case of community cohesion or a 'preference' on part of the Muslims to live together. A number of respondents claimed that communal politics and discrimination was responsible for their ghettoization. They argued that living together ensures physical safety and that the threat of violence had compelled them to migrate to these Muslim localities. This feeling was particularly strong in Mumbra because they were mostly victims of the 1992-93 riots of Mumbai. As one respondent put it "*What is the point living anywhere else (that is anywhere away from the Muslims) when our lives can be shattered any moment? The best example of it was Gujarat riots. What happened there? People who were very well established in business and professions were ruined overnight. And that is why Muslims have to stay together because if we are dispersed who will protect us? Even if we flourish outside but how long will that be for? A few years? A decade? A riot will happen and we will have to start from scratch. Why should we expose ourselves to such a risk? It is better for us to stay here*".

Apart from the security concern, there have been overt cases of discrimination in housing as well. During the interviews well-to-do professionals in Mumbra told us that Mumbra was not their first choice. They had looked for houses in other areas as well such Airoli and Nerul but once it was known that these people were Muslims, they were refused. One respondent narrated his experience "*I found this flat in Nerul which was in my budget. It was a fairly new building and I was quite keen on getting it. When the time to finalize the deal came and the agent heard my name, he told me straight away that no Muslims are allowed in this society. He wasn't even apologetic about it*".

The experience of being denied housing on the basis of their Muslim identity was fairly common to the households interviewed; either they themselves had been denied or knew of someone first-hand who was refused accommodation because his/her being a Muslim. The respondents also said that some of the estate-agents even justified this practice of refusing housing to Muslims. For example, some of the agents said that Muslims were dirty because they would slaughter animals and cook meat in the house. Some other agents said that since Muslims are connected with terrorists and criminals, it is not safe to provide them houses. However, the respondents pointed out that it was not the agents who were responsible but the property owners. In some cases, the agents had argued on behalf of their Muslim clients (that they should be allowed to rent/buy the flat) but the property owner had refused.

Health

The issue of health is of major concern in both Govandi and Mumbra. Apart from the obvious bodily harm caused by illness, it is also responsible for a double economic loss if it befalls the bread-winner. First, there is a loss of earnings caused by the inability to work. Second, the (meagre) savings are used up for treating it. This double-loss entailed as a consequence of poor health brings into sharp relief the importance of affordable healthcare. The following words of a respondent make it very clear how difficult it is for the poor to cope with diseases, "*Illness is a terrible thing. It should not happen to anyone and especially not to the poor. If we don't work, we will not have enough money for the treatment. On the other hand, if we do work while ill, the work will kill us. So, whether we work or not, it is death on either side*".

In Govandi, the people rely on a combination of both private and public health services but the primary source of the treatment for common illnesses was private practitioners. Of the households covered, 71 per cent of them went to private practitioners while only 29 per cent went to government clinics. They gave several reasons for visiting a private practitioner instead of the government clinic. For example, the queues and waiting time at the government clinics was much more, in their opinion the private practitioners were more thorough in their diagnosis unlike the government clinics where it was a rushed affair, the private practitioners were more easily accessible and at the time convenient to the patient, etc. Another reason for preferring private healthcare was that some of the respondents chose to be treated by alternative medicine such as *hakims*, *ayurveds*, etc.

However, the number of households preferring alternative medicine was not substantial (only 21%). Of those who went to alternative doctors, homoeopathy (11% of the households) was slightly preferred over *hakims/ayurveds* (7%). There were mainly two reasons for choosing alternative medicine. The first was that according to the respondents these alternative medicines did not have side-effects unlike modern medicines. The second reason was that these alternative doctors were cheaper than their modern counterparts (both consulting fees and the cost of the medicines).

As far as the case of surgeries and major illnesses is concerned, for its treatment the overwhelmingly majority (91%) in Govandi go to government hospital while only a small section (9%) goes to private hospitals. The reason provided by the respondents for this was that the private hospitals were simply unaffordable for surgeries and major diseases.[14]

Although the huge chunk of the population goes to the government hospital (called Shatabdi/Centenary Hospital), they are unhappy with it. It is ill-equipped to handle the number of cases that come to the hospital. It is a 210 bed hospital which serves a population of almost a million people (patients come from Govandi, Mankhurd, Trombay and Deonar). The Intensive Care Unit has almost ceased to be an ICU and has become an extension of the general ward. Moreover, a number of machines in the ICU are not functional. The hospital also lacks a blood bank. Furthermore, although the BMC has sanctioned the budget[15] for renovating the hospital, no work till now has been carried out. Consequently, a number of emergency cases are referred to Sion hospital. This leaves the residents of Govandi (and adjoining areas) very vulnerable in case of accidents or other emergencies which require immediate attention. The time which it takes to transfer patients from Shatabdi hospital to the Sion hospital could mean the difference between life and death.

The situation in Mumbra is even worse because there is no government hospital there. As a result, people have no option either to go to the private hospital[16] or to go to Kalwa (a town nearby) or some other place out of Mumbra. A section also comes to Mumbai for medical treatment. And most of these respondents chose to go to public hospitals. As far as the case of clinics is concerned, the majority of respondents said that they go to private doctors (and mostly those who practice modern medicine). So, the pattern of healthcare treatment in Govandi and Mumbra remains quite similar.

However, the more disturbing similarity between Govandi and Mumbra which emerged during the course of the study was the fact that the respondents complained that they had faced discrimination at the public hospitals (on the other hand, none of the respondents either from Govandi or Mumbra complained about being discriminated at private hospitals). A respondent from Govandi recalled the time when he was at the hospital because his wife was going to deliver his son. He recounted "*I was standing outside the room, when I overheard the mid-wife abusing my wife. She was saying that you Muslims keep producing children and all you bring are terrorists. I was shocked and deeply hurt by this.*" However, not all the patients are passive victims of discrimination. For instance, one respondent who had faced a similar experience reported the nurse to the superintendent. He said "*I was furious when I heard the nurse shout at my wife. So, I went to the superintendent and complained about it. I gave it in writing. I couldn't follow it because I didn't have the time. But I wanted to make a point that no one can do this. It is only when we* (Muslims) *assert our rights then we will be safe*".

The complaint about being discriminated against was not limited to their ill-treatment at hospitals alone. They also complained that the failure to renovate the Shatabdi hospital in Govandi and the absence of a government hospital in Mumbra was directly linked to the fact that most of the beneficiaries were Muslims. A resident of Govandi said, "*The government has allocated the money but nothing has happened. I know there is corruption but at least some money is spent. In our case, they haven't spent a single rupee. Why is this? You can figure it yourself.*" The respondents in Mumbra took a similar position, as one respondent said "*Even places smaller than Mumbra have hospitals... look at Kulwa for example but why not for Mumbra? They* (the Thane Municipal Corporation) *are deliberately neglecting us. They know that the population of Mumbra is mostly Muslim, so they do not build hospitals".*

Water

The residents of Govandi struggle everyday to ensure that they collect enough water to meet their needs. They are not successful everyday. Not surprisingly, water is a precious commodity in Govandi and the residents have to pay an exorbitant amount for it.

There is a 20-inch water main running along the Baji Prabhu Deshpande Road which carries the bulk of the water to the slums. From this main pipe the BMC has laid a single official connection to the other side of the road for every lane from where there is a distributory network. However, there are a number of illegal connections, both over-ground and underground, directly from the main pipe. These illegal connections are under the control of the 'water-mafia'. They have installed booster pumps and they draw the water out before it reaches its designated tap. So, it is only those who are living close to the main road who are able to get water from the municipality. The rest have to purchase water or get it from the water tanker. The residents usually buy water in two forms[17]. One is in the form of a jerry-can and the other is to pay a monthly amount to the water-mafia to get water for a certain time from the tap (for example 20 minutes a day). The rate for a jerry-can of 40 litres of water is between Rs. 15 to Rs. 20 while the rate for drawing water from a tap is around Rs. 450-500 a month for 20 minutes a day.

Of the households covered, 64 per cent relied mainly on the informal water market to meet their needs while 34 per cent were dependent on the water tanker. Only 2 per cent of the households declared handpump as the main source of water. Since the residents of Govandi have to buy water that too at such high rates (considering that BMC supplies water at only Rs. 2.25 per 1,000 litres[18]).

Water is also an area of concern for the residents of Mumbra but the situation is not as bad as Govandi. To begin with there is no 'water-mafia' (or at least in the form it exists in Govandi) and most of the people get their water supply from the municipality. The municipal water comes only for around one-and-a-half hours or two hours in a day which is inadequate for their needs. So, they supplement the Municipal water supply with bore-well water. It was also reported that because of numerous bore-wells the pressure of water coming from the taps falls causing inconvenience. Although the quality of the municipal water was satisfactory, sometimes the water-supply lines would get mixed with sewage water pipes causing muddy and dirty water to come through. In certain cases, water comes at very awkward times (around 4 or 5 a.m.) and in certain housing societies, the water supply was cut on Fridays. Here again the water-cut was seen as a sign of discriminatory attitude of the water department. As one respondent argued "*How come the same water department can supply us with water throughout the week except on Friday which is a holy day and we all bathe that day? They are well aware of what a water-cut on Friday entails and yet they indulge in this act. It is a reminder by them that they are powerful while we are helpless. It is not only in the case of water that this happens. A few years ago, they cut the electricity on the evening of Eid but there was no power-cut during the Ganesha festival. Isn't this a clear case of discrimination*"?

Sewage System and Garbage Disposal

The lack of an appropriate sewage system and garbage disposal mechanism is a serious problem in both Govandi and Mumbra. Govandi (particularly the Rafiq Nagar area) is built on a garbage dumping ground, so it does not come as a surprise that this has a severe waste management problem. However, the condition of Mumbra is not too heartening either. Virtually every open space is a garbage dump and even roads are littered with rubbish. The people have complained that the Thane Municipal Corporation (TMC) does not perform its duties properly. What happens is that the TMC sweeper comes and make heaps of the rubbish and leave. Later on, the TMC garbage truck arrives but the truck driver and his assistant refuse to put the garbage in the truck because they claim that it is the responsibility of the sweeper to load the garbage in the truck. Consequently, the people have employed private sweepers to load the garbage in the TMC truck. However, these private sweepers are usually employed by the housing societies and they are responsible for only their own particular housing society and at most the road outside. This still leaves the open areas neglected and there is no mechanism to clear away the trash which is dumped there. What makes the situation worse is that these are the same open areas where the children go out to play. When the locals were asked why they allowed the children to play in the filth, one of them responded "*They are kids and they feel like playing. We cannot keep them indoors all the time. And since there are no public parks or playgrounds for children to play, where else will they go*"?

The sewage system is also in a very bad shape. In Govandi, there are 7 major *nallas* (drains) and they are in a pathetic state. Most of them are open and emanate a very foul smell. The stench is overpowering and unbearable in most cases. What makes the situation worse is the fact that almost all the drains are clogged with garbage and the sewage water hardly flows. These stagnant pools of water then become breeding grounds for mosquitoes. This problem is especially very severe during the monsoons and people fall prey to malaria, dengue and other dangerous diseases which can easily be prevented if a proper drainage was in place.

The poor sewage system and garbage disposal poses a health hazard. In fact, a doctor in Mumbra said that "*People throw garbage everywhere and right out of their windows. They do not care about sanitation. This leads to a lot of health problems including jaundice, diarrhoea among others*". The improper sewage system is that in many instances it gets mixed with the water-supply lines and it contaminates the supply of clean water.

Another negative fallout of the inadequate drainage system is that it damages the roads (which to begin with are in a dismal state). The filthy water sometimes overflows on to the roads and at times so much that roads gets flooded.

Socio-Economic Status of Muslims in Govandi (and Mumbra)

Employment and Level of Education

The employment status[19] of the Muslims in Govandi presents a disheartening figure on a number of counts. Very few of them were employed in the organized sector of the economy. Only 0.2 per cent of those in the working age group were employed in government service[20] and 2.8 per cent were working in the private sector. However, none of those working in the private sector had a permanent job, they were low level executives and had temporary contracts. In other words, 99.5 per cent of those employed did not have a secured job.

The overwhelming majority of the people were working in the unorganised sector.[21] Of those working, 43.5 per cent were self-employed this was followed by those who were skilled labourers[22] (32.5 per cent).

However, it is important to bear in mind that these self-employed respondents are not high-end entrepreneurs but rather concentrated in petty trades such as small shopkeepers, street vendors, rag-picking, etc. Similarly, those who were skilled did not possess skills which had high-returns but were mostly skilled in occupations which had low returns, i.e., plumbing, electrician, tailor. The table on incomes of the sample population[23] gives an idea that they are mostly engaged in work with low earnings and not surprisingly their assets are very limited as well.

A clear gender was evident in the employment status of Muslims in Govandi. Although the average workforce participation rate (WPR)[24] was 47.3 per cent but it was heavily skewed towards men. The WPR for Muslim men was 77.6 per cent while for the Muslim women it was very low, that is, 15.5 per cent. These figures become starker when seen in absolute terms. Out of the 210 men in the age group of 15-60, there are 163 men who are working. On the other hand, out of the 200 women in the same age group only 31 are working. One reason for lower female WPR is that 39.5 per cent of them are full-time housewives.

Apart from the low WPR for women, they were concentrated in only a few occupations. In fact, there were no women who were in the government service and also there were no women who were skilled labourers.[25] Of those who were working, 48.3 per cent were home-based workers, this has an adverse impact on their mobility. So, in effect to begin with very few women were working (15.5 per cent) and of those who were working almost half (48.3 per cent) of them were located in home-based industries. Another important difference that emerged between men and women was in unemployment patterns.

The total percentage of men who were unemployed was 12.8 per cent while for women this figure almost half the workforce (49.5 per cent). However, the type of unemployment for men and women was different. Most of the men who were unemployed (85.1 per cent of the unemployed) were those who were seeking work but could not find work while only 14.9 per cent of the unemployed men were not looking work. Whereas for the women, the percentage of those who were unemployed and yet not looking for a job was quite high, both in absolute terms and relative terms (when compared with men). It stood at 53.5 per cent (while it was only 14.5 per cent for men). What becomes evident from this is that the compulsion to look for work outside the home is much more for men than for women. As one respondent (a lady) said, "*It is the man's responsibility to earn a living but it is not so for a woman. The thing is that when a girl or woman is at home, she is not sitting idle. She keeps doing some work but when men are at home, they just laze around*". This sentiment was echoed in a number of households. In other words, when a woman is not working, it is not perceived as unemployed but rather a conscious decision to stay at home. However, when a man is not working, it is seen as involuntary[26], that is, the man is just waiting for an opportunity to come by and he will start working. But this was not true for all households because 46.5 per cent of the unemployed women reported that they were seeking work but there was none available. This raises questions about the general misperception that Muslim women are not willing or allowed to work outside their homes.

It was on the question of employment that the respondents spoke at length about how discriminated the Muslims were as compared to the rest of the population. The common complaint was that the government did not make any provisions for employing Muslims but affirmative action existed for other marginalized communities such as scheduled castes and scheduled tribes. One respondent captured the sentiment when he said, "*The condition of the Muslims is as bad as dalits, if not worse, but nothing is done for us. The government simply ignores the plight of the Muslims. You have met so many people here already. Tell me how many have benefited from government jobs? Forget jobs, what about any government scheme? The fact is that the government is not interested in doing anything for the Muslims*".

It was not only the government which claimed to be discriminatory, many of the respondents said that the private sector was no better. They claimed that even private companies were not interested in hiring Muslims and especially residents of Govandi who are perceived as anti-social elements and criminals. One respondent (whose son was a sales agent for a private firm in Andheri) said "*Although my son is well-educated* (he was a commerce graduate), *he struggled to get a job. No one explicitly said that they refused his application because he was a Muslim and that too from Govandi but I am sure that was the reason. In one place, where his application was rejected, a class 12th pass-out was selected. Then a friend of mine in my home town* (a town in Bihar) *told me that his cousin's son had moved from Hyderabad to Mumbai and was working as a manager in a company in Andheri. I asked my son to get in touch with him and we were lucky because there were a few openings for salespersons in the company. Thanks to my friend's contact, my son got a job as a salesman. It would have been almost impossible to have gotten this job had the manager been non-Muslim*".

It indeed may be true that these Muslims might face discrimination during the selection process, especially for jobs in both the public and private sector at the lower rung where the jobs are given at the discretion of the higher officials. However, during the study it emerged that very few people had actually applied for jobs in the first place.

Out of those in the age group of 15-60 years, 91.1 per cent had not ever applied for a job either in the private or public sector. Here again, a gender divide is evident. The number of men who had applied for a job was more than two-and-a-half times than women (12.8% were men; and 5% were women). Another interesting fact which emerges when the data on job applications is disaggregated is that most of the applicants (73%) had applied for both private and government jobs whereas 27 per cent had applied only for private sector. However, there was not a single case of anyone who had only applied for a government job.

Two important reasons seem to be at play for the low-level of applications from the residents of Govandi. The first seems to be the low level of educational attainments (refer to table below) amongst the Muslims of Govandi. The second is the widespread and strong perception that since they are Muslims they will not get the job, hence, leading to self-exclusion.

A respondent narrated an instance of discrimination that his nephew (who also lives in Govandi) faced while trying to get a job as a police constable. He said, *"As you know very well there is a lot of corruption in the government, especially the police. To get a job in the government one has to bribe the officials involved. The rate for a police constable is Rs. 5 lakh. My nephew was able to arrange for the money with great difficulty. Anyway, so the agent* (the agent is the person who acts the go-between the prospective constable and the officials who will select him) *took him to the official responsible for his induction. The deal was almost finalized when the agent told the official the name of my nephew. On learning that he was a Muslim, the official got furious and abused the agent. He said, 'Why did you have to bring a landia* (a derogatory term used for Muslims)*? Couldn't you get someone of our own* (the reference was to some Marathi and Hindu)*? But finally, the official decided to accept the bribe and take my nephew in the force but my nephew refused. He said, 'It would have been impossible for me to work in such an environment'. So, you see there is a lot of anti-Muslim feeling and something should be done about this".*

What emerges from this incident is that even if Muslims have the capacity to pay their way to the job, they might not be willing to take it up because of the hostile attitude of others in the workforce.

In Mumbra that large number of the respondents was self-employed and was running small businesses. Here again a high concentration of Muslims in the unorganised sector was observed. One reason that came out very strongly for the prevalence of small businesses is found in the migration pattern of people to Mumbra. The population of Mumbra grew exponentially in the early years of 1990s after the Bombay riots. Muslims who had established businesses in Mumbai sold off all their property and migrated to Mumbra. When they came here they realized that the property was very cheap and that in the amount they had got from selling their houses, here they could buy a house as well as have money left for investing in businesses/shops. Since these respondents were running their own businesses and were in a Muslim locality (with mostly Muslim business partners and clientele), there were almost no complaints about being discriminated in their present occupation. But they repeated the same complaints as the residents of Mumbra that despite the poor condition of Muslims there was no affirmative action for them.

Economic Status, Assets and Documents Ownership

72.3 per cent of the sample population has per capita monthly income lower than Rs. 1,000 and only 3 per cent had a per capita monthly income of Rs. 2,500 or more. Ownership of fans and telephone/mobile phones was very high (100% and 91%) respectively. On the other hand, ownership of consumer durables was quite low (with the exception of TV which stood at 73%). Only 18 per cent of the households owned a fridge and only 2 per cent of the households possessed a computer. The ownership of motorcycles/scooters was also negligible with only 5 per cent households owning them.

Although a large share of the households (88%) did possess ration cards, few among them relied on the ration shops for their food supply. Even those who were BPL card holders (around 23%

of the households) informed that they were dependent on the market for meeting their food needs. One of the main reasons for going to the market was that the quality of the foodgrains at the ration shop was appalling. As one respondent put it, *"Brother, you are talking about ration shops? Do you even know the kind of stuff they sell? It is not fit even for animals"*. Therefore, the commodity which the people obtained regularly from the ration shop was kerosene.

Almost all the respondents spoke about the difficulties in obtaining these documents. The document which was the hardest to obtain was the passport. They said that out of all the government offices the police department is the most biased. Therefore, they create numerous hurdles in getting the passport. In the words of a respondent *"Passports are a gold-mine for the police-wallas. They know that whenever someone from Govandi is trying to get a passport, it is only for two reasons; either the person is going to the Gulf or is going for Hajj* (annual pilgrimage to Saudi Arabia). *In either case, the person is desperate to get the passport. The police exploit this situation. And you know how things are nowadays, they can deny the passport to any Muslim by framing him in some false case"*.

Another complaint regarding the documents was that the officials deliberately misspelt the names of the respondents. As one respondent recounted his experience at the ration card office, "*I submitted my form with the correct spelling of my name. Then to ensure that the official did not make a mistake, I told him my name not once or twice but thrice! And yet when I got my ration card, my name was misspelt*". The argument they put forward was that there were two reasons for doing so. The first was that it was to deliberately show that these officials did not know and also did not care about Muslim names. The second was that different spellings in separate documents means that it becomes difficult to cross-verify it. So, in case two identity proofs are required, the person despite having two ID proofs will not be able to use them because the names have been spelt differently in both cases.

While discussing about the documents it became evident that the respondents did not feel comfortable in government offices because the officials paid more attention to those who spoke Marathi. A respondent said, "*We rarely ever go to the office alone. We always take a Marathi friend along, that ensures that our work gets done smoothly. Otherwise there is no one who listens to a 'bhaiyya' (a derogatory term used for migrants from Bihar and Uttar Pradesh)*".

Banks and Access to Credit

It was observed in both Govandi and Mumbra that there was very limited financial inclusion. Not even half of the respondents in Govandi had a bank account (only 40% did). Furthermore, out of those who did possess bank accounts, very few of them were in the private sector (12%), the majority of them being in small local cooperative banks (53%).

However, the most disconcerting aspect of access to banking was despite the fact that over half the households had borrowed (55%), very few could avail loans and credit from formal institutions (1.8%). Most of the households had borrowed from informal sources, i.e., relatives and friends. This is more troubling in the light of the fact that 70 per cent of those save place their savings in the bank. So, what is happening is that the residents of Govandi are able to save in banks but are unable to borrow from them. One of the respondents said, "*I wanted to move my electrical shop to a bigger one. I approached a friend of mine who knew someone working in the bank. He helped me sort out the paper work and it was almost a done deal. And then nothing happened. Whenever I enquired about the status of my loan, the bank people would simply reply that it is in process. After a month of running around I gave up. Now, I am waiting for my brother to return from the Gulf and with his savings I will probably move to the new shop*".

Another important point was that most of the borrowings were for consumption purposes (92.8%) while only 7.2 per cent of the borrowings were for productive purposes (investment or for expanding business).

The situation of banks is pathetic in Mumbra as well. It was only two years ago that a bank opened in Mumbra. Furthermore, the residents of Mumbra do not get loans because Mumbra has been marked as a 'red zone'. One respondent (who was a central government employee in the stock exchange) said, "*One day in my office a manager of a public sector bank came. We talked for a while and then he offered that I should apply for a car loan and he will arrange for it. I told him that you will not give me the loan and he said that he will certainly get it. When I told him that I am from Mumbra, he became apologetic and said that then it won't be possible*".

Conclusion

This study was a humble endeavour to address the major lacunae in the existing literature on the socio-economic condition of Muslims in India which is the near absence of studies which look at the processes underlying the causes of Muslim poverty. Since this study was originally part of the researcher's master's thesis, there was a severe constraint on time and resources. Nonetheless, the study discusses a hitherto neglected area of research and it paves the way for further research on this topic. These future works can improve upon this study by taking larger sample sizes and covering in detail more than one Muslim-majority area. These studies can also be longitudinal which will capture the process of change operating in the area of studies. By carrying out such researches, it would be possible to draw generalizations about the poverty among Muslims of that region, if not India.[27]

Despite the constraints mentioned above, certain meaningful conclusions can be drawn from the study carried out in Govandi (and Mumbra). First, there is a strong sense of being discriminated against among the Muslims. Second, the macro-level findings of the Sachar Committee have been reaffirmed in this micro-level study. Third, the Muslim community of the area seems not have benefited from the high growth rates witnessed in the last decade and half which means that the idea of 'inclusive' growth needs to be reassessed.

Rampant Discrimination Meets Backwardness and Marginalization

Every single household of the study had reported being discriminated against at least once because of their Muslim identity. These cases ranged from being very serious such as the case of expecting mothers being abused by the hospital staff to minor incidents such as remarks being passed at in public places.

The feeling of being discriminated against was not only widespread but also intensely felt. Most of the respondents were very vocal about the issue of discrimination and would also talk at length about it. A number of them argued that the case of discrimination against Muslims is not limited to them or their surroundings alone. They pointed out that anti-Muslim sentiments are a global phenomenon and it is the hatred against Muslims which is responsible for the wars in Iraq and Afghanistan.

The failure of the government to provide adequate infrastructure and facilities, i.e., poor condition of hospitals, run-down schools, water problems and so forth is also perceived as a result of discrimination against Muslims. Most of the respondents felt that the abysmal conditions of their areas had a great deal to do with the fact that they were Muslims. Although they agreed that they were being ignored because they were poor and powerless but they also argued that they were worse off than the other communities. In other words, they admitted that other communities were also struggling for survival but none of them was in a state as bad as them. The most frequent comparison was with the scheduled castes where a large number of respondents said that their conditions were even worse than the Scheduled Castes. They also argued that the conditions of the scheduled castes had improved because they had the benefit of affirmative action.

A large number of respondents felt that Muslims should also be made beneficiaries of affirmative action. They pointed out that there was urgent need to grant them positive discrimination not only because they were poor but also because they were discriminated against. They also said that the limited affirmative action offered to them under the OBC quota was of little use because they were unable to get OBC certificates made. They further argued that there was too much competition in the OBC quota from other communities which were far advanced in both educational and economic terms.

They said that if affirmative action is brought in it will generate interest in education in Muslims because presently there is no incentive to carry on with higher education since jobs are not provided to Muslims. Some of them also spoke about the psychological confidence it will restore in the community, that is, it will make them feel that the government accepts the fact that Muslims are backward and discriminated against. The failure to provide affirmative action is equated with the failure to empathize with the plight of the community.

The sense of discrimination was so strong that there was a tendency to attribute almost all the events and incidents to their Muslim identity. So, for instance, a few respondents informed the researcher that the 'Bird Flu' breakout a few years ago was a conspiracy to destroy the businesses of the Muslim poultry farmers.

Although none of the government departments were perceived to be fair to the Muslims (although the army was praised for being impartial during riots), it was the police department which was considered the most biased. A number of the respondents were witness to the riots of 1992-93 and they claimed that the police always (not only during riots) takes an anti-Muslim position and misses no opportunity to harass them. The respondents also claimed that the youth of the area is at times picked up by the police and is framed in false criminal cases. Although the partial attitude of the police force is generally known what came as a surprise to the researcher was the information that pregnant Muslim women were ill-treated in public hospitals.

This research has focused on the self-perception of discrimination among Muslims, it is quite possible that some of these perceptions of discrimination may be extreme, as in the bird flu example stated above. However, it is important to address this sentiment of being discriminated against because it reflects a deep sense of alienation from the rest of the society.

The distance from remaining society is not only at a psychological level but also physical. However, this was not always the case. A number of the respondents who now live in this Muslim-dominated locality were living in mixed localities but it was after the riots of 1992-93 that they moved to Govandi (and Mumbra). What living together entails is that the community becomes physically secure, that is, from the threat of riots but it also results in them being easy targets of discrimination by the authorities. The respondents argued that this part of a larger conspiracy of the Hindu right-wing to force them ghettoes and then denying them basic services. They said that the right-wing was unleashing indirect violence on them. The Muslim areas are identified as 'mini-Pakistans' and the government can simply under-serve these areas, if not deprive them completely of public services.

In brief, the Muslims suffer from a combination of backwardness, marginalization (both political and economic) and discrimination. As far as backwardness and marginalization are concerned, they both are easily observable, i.e., backwardness in education, low presence in decision-making bodies, etc. However, capturing discrimination is much more challenging. The important point to realize is that these three factors—backwardness, marginalization and discrimination are deeply enmeshed together and it is difficult to isolate them from each other. Therefore, there is a need for further micro-level studies from which it might become possible to identify not only the discrimination **perceived** by Muslims but also **actually** faced by them.

Sachar Committee Report Findings Reaffirmed

The findings of this research reaffirmed the information that the Sachar Committee had gathered at the national level. For instance, most of the households covered were engaged in the informal sector of the economy and employment in the organized sector was negligible. According to the Sachar Committee, this is the case at the national level as well. Almost three-quarters of urban Muslim workers in India are in the unorganized sectors. The low workforce participation rates of Muslim women which were observed during the study of Govandi are also a national trend.

The Sachar Committee had also pointed that in villages there was an inverse relationship between the population of Muslims and the public services available to them. Although the setting of this study was urban, it was poorly served by public services and infrastructure. However, considering that Govandi was a slum area, so the lack of adequate services should not come as a surprise. The Sachar Committee had also pointed out that the proportion of Muslim households living in **pucca** houses was lower than the total population. It also showed that over half the population did not have access to toilets. The living conditions of the residents were worse.

The report had also pointed out to the high incidence of urban poverty among Indian Muslims. In the case of Govandi as well the respondents reported very low incomes. Although very limited data on the educational status of the residents of Govandi could be collected but it displayed the same pattern which is observed at the national level, i.e., high rate of illiteracy, very few graduates, etc. In Govandi, the respondents also struggled to get credit from formal institutions. This was reported to be a serious problem by the Sachar Committee, it also pointed out how a number of areas with high concentration of Muslim population were earmarked as 'negative zones', Govandi is one of those areas.

Inclusive or Exclusive Growth?

India is the second-fastest growing economy in the world and according to the Economic Survey of 2011-12, the growth rate is expected to reach 9 per cent. Although India has maintained rapid growth rates in the last decade and half, it has been unsuccessful in eliminating poverty. This in turn raises the question whether all sections of society are benefiting from the high growth rates or not. In other words, the question is whether this growth is 'inclusive' or 'exclusive'.

From the data available from the Sachar Committee which shows widespread poverty among Muslims especially urban Muslims and from the findings of this study, it seems that the Muslims have been excluded from the 'growth story' of India. Therefore, it is essential that such policies are designed which makes growth 'inclusive' and allows all sections of the society, including Muslims, to gain from it. However, it is important to recall the **nature** of the present growth model. It is based on a liberalized economic environment which gives greater autonomy to market forces and is largely driven by the private sector. Since the market forces cannot ensure fair and equitable distribution of resources, it is of critical importance that the State plays a proactive role in not only ensuring high growth rates but also its equitable distribution. The responsibility of improving the socio-economic condition of the population including the deprived Muslim community lies with the State and it cannot be left to the vagaries of the market. In other words, if this 'exclusive' growth has to become 'inclusive', it would require active intervention on the part of State apparatus.

What Should Be Done

Drawing upon Sen's distinction between the **intrinsic** and the **instrumental**[28], it can be argued that the exclusion of Muslim is both. It is intrinsically appalling because in a secular and democratic country like India, no group should be excluded, least of all on the basis of religion. The problems and challenges faced by the Muslims of Govandi are numerous and tough. This is not only because of their Muslim identity but also their poverty.

However, there is no magic bullet which can solve such a complicated problem, that is, the deprivation of Muslims. Therefore, the appropriate response of the authorities should be to adopt a multi-pronged approach which tackles both general (i.e., provision of adequate health services) and community-specific issues (i.e., sense of discrimination). The authorities will also have to collaborate with already existing organizations, especially community-based ones, working in these areas. As it becomes evident from people's responses, there is a significant degree of 'trust deficit' between the community and the government. Therefore, before any initiative is undertaken, the authorities must take the community into confidence.

Nonetheless, it is a matter of grave concern that there has been considerable delay in taking action which addresses the poverty of Muslims. It has been over half a decade since the constitution of the Sachar Committee. The fact of the matter is, as the Sachar Committee itself pointed out, that the community is tired of presenting memorandums and reports; it looks forward to meaningful and concrete action.

Table 13.1: State-wise Profile of Sample Households

Home State	*No. of Sample Households*	*No. of Sample Population*
Uttar Pradesh	51	321
Bihar	49	279

Table 13.2: Age-wise Profile of Sample Households

Age Group of Sample Pop.	*Percentage of Male Sample Pop.*	*Percentage of Female Sample Pop.*	*Percentage of Total Sample Pop.*
0-5	6.8	9.8	8.3
6-14	17.3	15.9	16.7
15-60	68.6	68.00	68.3
Above 60	7.1	6.1	6.7

Table 13.3: Housing Type

Housing Type	*Percentage of Sample Households*
Slums/Chawls	86
Flats	14

Table 13.4: Persons per Room

No. of Persons per Room	*Percentage of Sample Households*
3 or less	24
4 to 6	69
7 or more	7

Table 13.5: Facilities inside the House

Facility Inside the House	*Percentage of Sample Households*
Toilet Facility	33
Bathroom Facility	71

Table 13.6: Ownership of House

Ownership of House	*Percentage of Sample Households*
Owned	64
Rented	36

Table 13.7: Primary Source of Medical Treatment for Common Diseases

Medical Treatment – Common Diseases (Primary Source)	*Percentage of Sample Households*
Private	71
Government	29

Table 13.8: Type of Medical Treatment

Medical Treatment (Type)	*Percentage of Sample Households*
Modern (Western) Medicine	79
Homoeopathic	11
Hakim/Ayurvedic	7
Others	3

Table 13.9: Primary Source of Medical Treatment—Surgery/Major Illness

Medical Treatment – Surgery/Major Illness (Primary Source)	*Percentage of Sample Households*
Private	9
Government	91

Table 13.10: Primary Source of Water Supply

Water Supply (Primary Source)	*Percentage of Sample Households*
Informal Water Market	64
Tanker	34
Handpump	2

Table 13.11: Permanent Job Holders: Sector-wise Breakup

Permanent Jobs	*Male (%age of those in 15-60 age group)*	*Female (%age of those in 15-60 age group)*	*Total (%age of those in 15-60 age group)*
Public Sector	0.4	0	0.2
Private Sector	0	0	0

Table 13.12: Occupational Patterns of those in 15—60 years Age Group

Occupation	*Male (%age of those in 15-60 age group)*	*Female (%age of those in 15-60 age group)*	*Total (%age of those in 15-60 age group)*
Skilled Labour	25.2	0	12.9
Self-Employed	33.8	4.5	19.5
Home-based Workers	2.8	7.5	5.1
Manual/Unskilled Labour	7.1	1	4.1
Private Sector Employee	1.9	1	2.8
Government Service	0.4	0	0.2
Housewives	0	39.5	19.2
Students	9.5	11	10.2
Others	6.9	1.5	3.9
Involuntary Unemployment	10.9	23	16.8
Voluntary Unemployed*	1.9	26.5	13.9

* **Voluntary Unemployment**— Those who are unemployed but are not looking for work.

Table 13.13: Distribution in Occupation those who were Employed and Working

Occupation	*Male (%age of those employed)*	*Female (%age of those employed)*	*Total (%age of those employed)*
Skilled Labour	32.5	0	27.3
Self-Employed	43.5	29	41.2
Home-based Workers	3.6	48.3	10.8
Manual Labour	9.2	6.4	8.7
Private Sector Employee	2.4	6.4	3.0
Government Service	0.6	0	0.5
Others	7.9	9.6	8.2

Table 13.14: Workforce Participation Rate

	Male	*Female*	*Total*
Workforce Participation Rate	77.6	15.5	47.3

Table 13.15: Applications for Jobs

Applied for Jobs	*Male (%age of those in 15-60 age group)*	*Female (%age of those in 15-60 age group)*	*Total (%age of those in 15-60 age group)*
Either Pvt or Govt	12.8	5	8.9
Did Not Apply	87.2	95	91.1

Table 13.16: Application for Jobs-Breakdown

Job Applications (Breakdown)	*Male (%age of those in 15-60 age group)*	*Female (%age of those in 15-60 age group)*	*Total (%age of those in 15-60 age group)*
Total Applications	12.8	5	8.9
Both Pvt and Govt	9	4	6.5
Only Private	3.8	1	2.4
Only Government	0	0	0

Table 13.17: Level of Education

Level of Education	*Percentage of Male Sample Pop.*	*Percentage of Female Sample Pop.*	*Percentage of Sample Population*
Illiterate	11.9	16.9	14.3
Less than Primary	34.0	39.2	36.5
Primary to Secondary	38.5	37.7	38.1
Higher Secondary	8.7	3.7	6.3
Graduation (All Streams)	2.4	1.1	1.8
Technical (ITI/Diploma)	4.2	1.1	2.7

Table 13.18: Monthly Per Capita Income

Per Capita Income (Monthly)	*Percentage of Sample Population*
591 or less	43.8
592 to 999	28.5
1000 to 1499	11.0
1500 to 1999	7.6
2000 to 2499	2.1
2500 or more	3.0

Table 13.19: Possession and Assets

Possessions/Assets	Percentage of Sample Households
Fan	100
Telephone/Mobile	91
Kerosene Stove	54
Cooking Gas	46
Fridge	18
Motorbike/Scooter/Moped	5
Computer	2

Table 13.20: Ownership of Documents

Documents	Percentage of Sample Households
Ration Card	88
Electoral Card	79
Driving Licence	55
Pan Card	54
BPL Card	23
Passport	21

Table 13.21: Bank Account Holders

Bank Account (Holders)	Percentage of Sample Households
Households with bank accounts	40
Households without bank accounts	60

Table 13.22: Bank Account Type

Bank Account (Type)	Percentage of Sample Households (who have bank accounts)
Cooperatives	53
Public Sector	30
Private Sector	12
Others	5

Table 13.23: Level of Indebtedness

Level of Indebtedness	Percentage of Sample Households
Debt-free	45
Rs. 10,000 or less	16
Rs. 10,001 to Rs. 25,000	26
Rs. 25,001 or more	13

Table 13.24: Sources of Debt

Sources of Debt	Percentage of Sample Households (of those who borrowed)
Relatives	63.6
Friends/Associates	29.1
Formal Institutions (Banks/Credit Societies)	1.8
Others	5.5

Table 13.25: Location of Savings

Location of Savings	*Percentage of Sample Households*
No Savings	50
Banks	35
Home	10
Others	5

Table 13.26: Reasons for Borrowing

Reasons for Borrowing	*Percentage of Sample Households (of those who borrowed)*
Healthcare	41.8
Wedding/Ceremonial Purposes	20.0
Purchase House	16.3
Consumer Durables	14.5
Business Expansion/Other Investment	7.2

REFERENCES

Bharucha, R.N. 2006. *Yamuna Weeps Gently: A Journey into the Yamuna Pushta Slum Demolitions*. Sainathan Communication, New Delhi.

DNA. 2010. *BMC's Outstanding Water Supply Dues*, (October 6, 2010) (http://www.dnaindia.com/mumbai/report_bmc-s-outstanding-water-supply-dues-rs3065-crore_1448272 Accessed on 9th November 2010)

Dobbin, Christine. 1972. *Urban Leadership in Western India: Politics and Communities in Bombay City, 1840-1885*. Oxford University Press, Oxford.

Government of India. 2006. *Social, Economic and Educational Status of Muslim Community in India: A Report* (Sachar Committee), Prime Minister's High Level Committee, New Delhi.

John, Rijo and Rohit Mutatkar. 2005. "State-wise Estimates of Poverty among Religious Groups in India", *Economic and Political Weekly* (March 23).

Khalidi, Omar. 2005. *Muslims in Indian Economy.* Three Essays Collective, New Delhi.

Khan, Sameera. 2007. "Negotiating the Mohalla: Exclusion, Identity and Muslim Women in Mumbai", *Economic and Political Weekly,* (April 28)

Sen, Amartya. 1999. *Development as Freedom.* A.A. Knopf, New York.

Sharrif, Abu Saleh. 1995. "Socio-Economic and Demographic Differentials between Hindus and Muslims in India", *Economic and Political Weekly* (November 18).

Wilkinson, Steven. 2007. "A Comment on the Analysis in Sachar Report", *Economic and Political Weekly* (March 10)

NOTES

1. In 1871, the share of Muslims in the population in Bombay was 15 per cent but there were only 9 per cent Muslims in the public services. By 1886, their share in the population had increased to 18.3 per cent but there were only 5.4 per cent Muslims in the Executive and Judicial Services. (Khalidi, 2005, pp. 19-22)
2. Dobbin (1972), p. 229.
3. Government of India (Sachar Committee Report, 2006) pp. 265-267.
4. Government of India (Sachar Committee Report, 2006) pp. 367-368.
5. John and Mutatkar (2005, p. 1337) write "prevalence, depth and severity of poverty is highest among Muslims in urban areas".
6. Wilkinson (2007), p. 832.
7. Shariff (1995), p. 2953.
8. The data in this section "Brief Introduction of Govandi and Mumbra" is from the report commissioned by the Maharashtra State Minorities Commission entitled *Socio-Economic and Educational Status of Muslims in Mumbai* (2009) unless otherwise stated.
9. This information was obtained from the corporator's office of ward no. 113, Mumbra.
10. *Hindustan Times*, *Times of India* and DNA.
11. This data has been presented in tabular form at the end of this chapter.
12. Quoted in Bharucha (2006), p. 179.
13. This is not to argue that the living conditions as a whole are better for the residents of Mumbra. The residents of Mumbra also suffer from the lack of adequate infrastructure; it is only that the housing conditions are better. In certain instances (e.g., roads), the conditions are much worse in Mumbra.
14. It is important to keep in mind that even for common illnesses, it is not easy for the poor to afford private doctors. The reason for visiting private practitioners is not so much as choice as is the fact that in the absence of well-equipped and effective public healthcare system, the respondents were forced to go to private practitioners at a very high cost.

15. *Hindustan Times*, No Funds to Upgrade Govandi Hospital, (March 20, 2010) (http://www.hindustantimes.com/News-Feed/mumbai/No-funds-to-upgrade-Govandi-hospital/Article1-521136.aspx Accessed on 28th November, 2010)
16. The name of the private hospital is Kalsekar. It is quite well-equipped and big but is not large enough to meet the needs of entire Mumbra. Furthermore, everybody cannot afford to be treated there.
17. The author has labelled these two forms as the informal water market in the Table 1.8.
18. Rate listed in DNA (2010) *BMC's Outstanding Water Supply Dues*, (October 6, 2010) (http://www.dnaindia.com/mumbai/report_bmc-s-outstanding-water-supply-dues-rs3065-crore_1448272 Accessed on 9th November, 2010).
19. This has been gathered using Usual Principal Status (UPS). It has a reference period of one year and those who have worked for 6 months or more are considered as employed. Although the employment pattern of those in the unorganized sector is very complex, for the purposes of this study, the worker has been assigned that employed category in which s/he claimed to have worked the most number of days during the period of his/her employment. For example, if a person has worked for 9 months in the year out of which s/he has worked for 6 months as a manual labourer and 3 months as a home-based worker, s/he shall be categorized as a manual labourer. Although this method is rather crude but it was the best that could be managed within the constraints of time and resources.
20. In absolute terms, there was only one person was employed in the government. He was a lower-division clerk in the Municipal Corporation.
21. Although the precise definition of the unorganized sector remains contested, for the purposes of this study it has been defined as those enterprises whose activities or collection of data is not regulated under any legal provision or do not maintain any regular accounts and contractual labour agreements are absent.
22. These are skilled workers (electricians/plumbers/mechanics/carpenters/tailors and others) who are employed by someone else, usually in a shop owned by someone else and are paid every month. Those skilled workers who do not work for others are included in the self-employed category. Although it is true that it is not possible to draw a sharp distinction between the skilled labourers who are employees and self-employed, because the skilled employees also carry out extra independent work.
23. It should be clarified that an exhaustive consumption expenditure survey was not undertaken to arrive at these figures. These are the figures given by the respondents themselves. Keeping in mind the tendency for incomes to be underreported, these figures are quite likely to be underestimated.

24. The WPR has been defined as the ratio between the number of workers in the age group 15-60 years and the total population of that age group.
25. One category of women who could have been included in skilled workers could have been women doing embroidery work. These women have been included in the home-based category because they work from homes, usually they get the cloth and the design from outside and then they carry out the work at home.
26. **Involuntary Unemployment** = Those who are unemployed and are looking for work.
27. It is heartening to note that the Tata Institute of Social Sciences (TISS) has initiated 'Transforming M-Ward' project which seeks to reduce the Infant Mortality Rate of this ward. Govandi falls under this ward and constitutes a sizeable chunk of this ward. TISS has carried out a large scale household and community amenities survey of this area which will possibly provide us with greater insight into the situation of Muslims in this area. The author was part of this project. For further details of this project, visit http://platinum.tiss.edu/the-m-ward-initiative
28. Sen (1999).

14

Muslims of India: Expectations from the Twelfth Plan

Maulana Mohammad Fazlur Rahim Mujaddidi

Developmental attention to the issues of minorities, received special attention in the Eleventh Five Year Plan, which was preceded by the setting up of the Ministry of Minority Affairs as the nodal agency for the welfare and development of minorities. It was soon followed by the inauguration of the Prime Minister's 15-Point Programme for the welfare of minorities.

The Eleventh Plan looked at certain operational strategies for the uplift of minorities. It decided to adopt an area-based approach, and according to the Census of 2001, 1,228 community development blocks were identified. 338 Class towns, and 156 districts having minority population of 25 per cent and above were also identified and it was decided to launch both infrastructure development and beneficiary oriented programmes in these places.

However, at present there is a great disparity in the demand and the resource availability, which further increases the gap between Muslims and other socio-religious groups. For example, if we look at the budgetary provisions for the schemes for the welfare of children in the year 2008-09, under 18 years, we find that the share of children belonging to the Scheduled Castes was 52 per cent of the total allocations, while it was 40 per cent for the Scheduled Tribes. But it was a mere 8 per cent for the Minorities. Such disparities call for immediate remedial action in the interest of equity and in the national interest.

It has also been observed that there is another discriminatory dimension to backwardness, as it has some relationship with Muslim concentration in an area. In the population, as Muslim concentration increases, it generally has a negative effect on the literacy levels (Tables 14.1 and 14.2).

Table 14.1: The Four Sstates W.B, U.P., Bihar, Assam having more than Half of the Total Muslim Population seem to be responsible for decline in Literacy

Literacy Rate				Muslim %	States	% of Muslim Reside Here	Muslim Literacy Rate Difference		
Hindus	SC/ST	Muslims	Rest Others				Others	Hindus	SC/ST
65.1	52.2	59.10	70.80	13.44	All India	100.00	−11.70	−6.00	6.90
72.4	56.1	57.50	81.60	25.25	W.B	14.66	−24	−15	1
58.0	46.2	47.80	62.20	18.50	U.P.	22.27	−14	−10	2
47.9	28.5	42.00	52.60	16.53	Bihar	9.94	−11	−6	14
70.0	64.0	48.40	71.30	30.92	Assam	5.97	−23	−22	−16
62.7	**49.4**	**50.96**	**67.70**		**Total**	**52.84**	**−17**	**−12**	**2**
72.0	62.1	82.90	75.80	5.56	T.N.	2.51	7	11	21
65.6	51.5	70.10	71.10	12.23	Kamataka	4.68	−1	5	19
59.4	48.9	68.00	63.30	9.17	A.P.	5.06	5	9	19
90.2	80.8	89.40	93.10	24.70	Kerala	5.70	−4	−1	9
71.8	**60.8**	**77.60**	**75.83**		**Total**	**17.95**	**2**	**6**	**17**

Source: Based on Sachar Committee Report.

Table 14.2: Districts with Highest and Lowest Muslim Population

10 Districts with Highest Muslim Population (All are in MCDs List)				10 Districts with Lowest Muslim Population (Non-MCDs)			
	Districts	Muslim Population per cent	Muslims Literacy Rate %		Districts	Muslim Population per cent	Muslim Literacy Rate %
1	Rampur	49	33	1	Lalitpura	3	66
2	Moradabad	46	36	2	Chitrakoot*	4	66
3	Bijnor	42	50	3	Mainpuri	5	49
4	J.P. Nagar	39	43	4	Sonbhadra	5	59
5	Saharanpur	39	48	5	Ballia	7	67
6	Muzaffar Nagar	38	46	6	Mahoba*	7	62
7	Balrampur*	37	35	7	Auraiya*	7	59
8	Bahraich	35	33	8	Etawah	7	57
9	Bareilly	34	37	9	Jhansi	7	67
10	Meerut	33	46	10	Mirzapur	7	54

If we look at the conditions within a State. e.g., Assam: we find that as the percentage of Muslims decreases in a parliamentary constituency, the literacy levels indicate a corresponding increase (Table 14.3).

Table 14.3: Decrease in the Muslims Percentage and increase of Literacy Level in a Perliamentary Constitutency of Assam

Social Indicators 2008	Muslim %	PARTY WON	Literacy Rate	Female Literacy Rate	Primary School Pupil Teacher Ratio	Primary School Drop-out Rate	Fully Immunized Children
All India	14		72	62	66	19	46
Assam	33		69	61	41	50	37
Dhubri	71	AUDF	57	50	103	48	25
Karimganj (SC)	57	INC	69	62	68	62	9
Nowgong	52	BJP	66	59	30	45	33
Barpeta	51	INC	65	57	76	27	27
Silchar	37	BJP	73	66	63	35	–5
Mangaldoi	36	BJP	66	58	43	33	24
Kokrajhar (ST)	35	BPF	63	55	64	25	22
Kaliabor	29	INC	72	65	44	34	46
Gauhati	28	BJP	78	71	19	19	79
Tezpur	18	AGP	67	58	66	88	63
Lakhimpur	9	INC	71	62	31	24	36
Jorhat	7	INC	81	74	23	59	46
Dibrugarh	4	INC	72	63	53	35	29
Autonomous District (ST)	3	INC	66	57	113	40	18

Source: ET-Indicus Analytics 2008.

Similarly if we look at the States of India, we find that as the population of Muslims in a State increases, it leads to a corresponding decrease in number of colleges per thousand persons (Table 14.4).

Table 14.4: Increase in the Muslims Population and decrease in Number of Colleges

Population	*Muslims*	*No. of*		*State*	*Seat/ Population In Number*	*College/ Population In Lakhs*
In Lakhs		*Colleges*	*Seats*			
624	35	254	80,417	Tamil Nadu	776	2.46
762	70	236	82,970	Andhra	919	3.23
310	79	80	24,413	Kerala & Lakshadweep	1,304	3.58
529	65	118	46,375	Karnataka	1,140	4.48
969	103	155	48,250	Maharashtra	2,008	6.25
368	8	41	13,014	Orissa	2,828	8.98
85	10	9	1,440	Uttaranchal	5,895	9.43
603	38	61	20,210	Madhya Pradesh	2,986	9.89
507	46	37	12,965	Gujarat	3,908	13.69
565	48	41	15,045	Rajasthan	3,756	13.78
802	202	54	15,477	West Bengal	5,180	14.85
1662	307	89	28,953	Uttar Pradesh	5,740	18.67
269	37	10	3,385	Jharkhand	7,960	26.95
267	82	3	750	Assam	35,541	88.85
830	137	8	1,905	Bihar	43,569	103.75

Muslim concentration areas seem to register very low levels of development. Education levels are so depressing among the poor Muslims that after security, it emerges as the second most important issue besieging the community. Muslims are behind other minorities like Jains, Sikhs and Christians in terms of enrolment and are much behind when it comes to looking at the relative figures of these communities in terms of students who complete graduation (Fig. 14.1). It shows an alarming dropout rate.

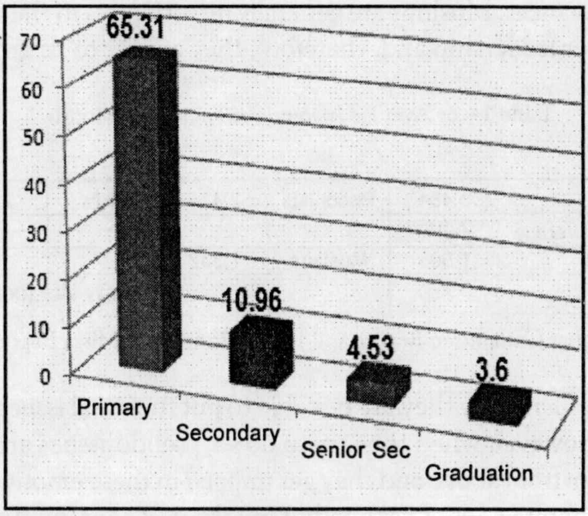

Fig. 14.1

Source: Justice Ranganath Mishra Report.

Out of every 100 Muslim students enrolled, only 65 reach the primary level, and by the time they reach graduation level, the figure drops to 3.6 per cent (Table 14.5).

Table 14.5: Percentage of Dropout Muslim Students at Primary and Graduation Level

Level	*Percentage*	*Dropout Percentage*
Primary	65.31	—
Secondary	10.96	54.35
Senior Secondary	4.53	60.78
Graduation	3.60	61.71

Source: Justice Ranganath Mishra Report.

As regards, the economic status of Muslims, it is again less than the national average, and lower than all the other minorities (Table 14.6).

The present existential state of the community has led to the creation of great despair among them and they do not know as to where they are headed and whom to approach for the redressal of their grievances. Muslims are generally directionless in the absence of a proper leadership and, therefore, they appear to be groping in

Table 14.6: Average Income Per Family per Month

(In Rs.)

Parsis	3,484	Buddhists	2,478	Sikhs	2,285
National Average	2,103				
Christians	1;906	Muslims	1,832		
				Family size (nearly 4)	

Source: Sachar Committee Report and Justice Ranganath Misra Report.

darkness. Generally they are not able to put their real issues on the agenda, however, when they try to do so, pseudo-issues are thrust upon them from above and they get trapped in these emotive issues which generate a lot of passion but are short of content. To add to the woes, the Government has created more confusion by not responding adequately to the problems of Muslims, and whatever schemes have been floated, they are deficient, to say the least. Moreover, the implementation of these schemes leaves a lot to be desired.

Suggestions of Sachar Committee and their Implementation: Most of the recommendations of the Sachar Committee have been ignored by the Government. The Sachar Committee recommended that a National Data Bank be created where all relevant data pertaining to the socio-economic and educational status of different Socio-Religious Communities is maintained. However, although the concerned Ministries and Departments claim that NBD is ready, welfare data of schemes is available in general and total form. Not a single welfare data of schemes is linked with beneficiaries of the schemes. Since nothing is clear in this respect, it has led to the creation of a state of confusion in the community as regards welfare schemes of the Government.

The Sachar Committee also recommended that an Autonomous Assessment and Monitoring Authority (AAMA) be set-up, to evaluate the extent of developmental benefits that accrue to the different SRC's through various programmes. However, it is said that AAMA has been established in the Planning Commission, but no one outside knows the activities of the AAMA. Not even a single meeting of the AAMA has been held since its creation with public participants.

It was also suggested that more access to credit and governmental schemes be made available to Muslims, but a lot needs to be done in this regard as well. Moreover, education was earmarked as the top priority area, but it still is not the favoured area of the designers of welfare schemes. The utilization of the Multi-Sectoral Development Fund bears ample testimony to this. As per Ministry of Minority Affairs report dated 31-12-2009, projects worth Rs. 1,589 crore have been approved by the Ministry as Central Government share. Out of this Rs. 615 crore has been used in Indira Awas Yojana (IAY). This comes to 40 per cent of the total utilization. Since, IAY is already covered under PM's 15-point programme, it means that the above 40 per cent of the funds have been transferred to the PM's 15-point programme. Moreover, IAY has its own parameters of utilization, where 60 per cent of the total IAY allocation should be utilized for the construction/upgradation of dwelling units of the SC/ST/BPL households. What would be left for the minorities in a scheme apparently running in their names. This is an open testimony to the sincerity of the powers that be. In Assam, IAY fund allocation is more than 80 per cent of total funds allocated to Assam. Although Assam has 7 per cent SC population and 12 per cent ST population, as against 33 per cent Muslims.

Centrally Sponsored Schemes: The condition of implementation of centrally sponsored schemes also calls for greater attention. For example, an outlay of Rs. 325 crore has been provided for the revised scheme for providing quality education in Madarsas for the Eleventh Plan period, but only 10 per cent funds of this scheme have been utilized. Because of heavy non-utilization no extra funds would be allocated in the Twelfth Plan.

The SC/ST/OBCs are getting the scholarship support since long, the Minority students' scholarship has been introduced in 2007. Although the Ministry of Minority Affairs intends to progressively increase the number of scholarships for Muslim students, but despite the best stated intentions the numbers actually disbursed, do not cater the needs of even 1 per cent of Muslim children up to Senior Secondary.

There are different hurdles which Muslims face in relation to the available scholarships. The delivery mechanism is cumbersome, complicated and costly. In spite of clear instructions from the Government, several nationalized banks are not willing to allow opening of accounts with zero balance, they insist on a deposit, which often poor Muslims cannot afford. Another difficulty is in obtaining the income certificate, as eventually these certificates are to be issued by the lower bureaucracy, whose integrity and discriminatory attitude is hidden to none. Moreover, the form runs into 5-6 pages, and the schools and colleges are reluctant to fill the columns in the forms, thus often rendering them incomplete and worthy of rejection. Then there is a particular time-period within which the forms should be filled. So to keep track when these forms come and then to meet the deadline, along with the above-mentioned requirements, makes it a hard nut to crack. Also, for minority students the awarded scholarship is discontinued if a student fails to secure 50 per cent marks or equivalent grade in the last final examination. No such condition is there for SC and ST students. What is required is that the norms of these scholarships should be brought at par with the scholarships for students belonging to the Scheduled Castes and Tribes, which are fully centrally sponsored and available round the year. Moreover, if we look at the Eleventh Five Year Plan outlays, we find that Minorities got less allocation, which was followed by less utilization as well (Table 14.7).

For example, SC students who were 16.66 crore, got Rs. 5,196 crore, whereas, Minority students who were 19.37 crore, got Rs. 3,150 crore. The utilization as regards Minorities was 49 per cent and as regards SCs it was 95 per cent.

It has been observed that the Government does not care much for issues of Muslims, but becomes active once it feels that these issues would impact the general development of the country.

What the Muslims need to do is to have a strategy of competing more gainfully in the game of political power in India. The Government must be pressurized to give more equitable representation to Muslims in administration. The feeling of discriminatory justice which has crept in the community because

Table 14.7: Eleventh Five Year Plan—Less Allocation followed by Less Utilization

(Amounts in Crore)

Minority Welfare Scholarship	*XI Plan Outlay*	*3 Years (2007-10)*		*Budget Allocation 2010-11*	*4 years (2007-11)*	
		Exp.	*% Utilisation*		**Exp.*	*% Utilisation*
Post Matric	1150	230	20	265	495	43
Merit Cum Means	600	203	34	135	338	56
Pre-Matric	1400	265	19	450	715	51
Total	**3150**	**698**	**22**	**850**	**1548**	**49**

of happenings in the past, needs to be set right. Informed sections in the community must open channels for dialogue with the Government on substantive issue, like reservation for Muslims. The community needs to be sensitized of the various schemes of the Government and how they could make best use of it.

Expectations from Twelfth Plan: With all the evidence as regards backwardness of Minorities before the Government, there still appears to be some reluctance in allocating funds for their uplift. For the year 2010-11, the amount assigned per head for the Minorities is Rs. 138, while for the SCs it is Rs. 1,228 and for the STs, it is Rs. 1,450. Hence, Minorities would continue to lag behind.

The budgetary allocations for the Minorities need to be enhanced by at least 10 times. Presently the allocations are meagre and they too are not properly utilized. For example, in the Eleventh Plan, the outlay was Rs. 1,400 crore, out of which only Rs. 487 crore were used up in the first four years, i.e., up to 2010-11, which comes to only about 35 per cent of the total amount allocated.

In the case of Post-Matric scholarships Rs. 1,150 crore were allocated and in the first four years only Rs. 388 crore were utilized, which also comes to about 34 per cent of the total allocation. For the Merit-cum-Means scholarship Rs. 600 crore were allocated, out of which Rs. 253 crore were utilized, i.e., about 42 per cent of the total allocation.

The top-most priority needs to be education. At least 75 per cent of the total budgetary allocations for Minorities should be earmarked for education. All scholarship norms should be at par with SC/ST scholarship norms. The Ministry of Minority Affairs should concentrate only on scholarships for minorities. The domain of the 15-Point programme should be expanded to include urban welfare schemes also. Micro-financing from Government institutions and PSU bank schemes related to Minority Groups should be further segregated among different Minority Groups, as has been done in relation to scholarship programmes.

MCD projects/funds should be further divided into Block level and Minority concentration Blocks should be identified. Moreover, educational infrastructure development should be given the highest priority in the remaining funds of MCD. The resource allocations for Minorities should be made non-lapsable, and the unspent money should be carried forward for developing educational infrastructure. In all schemes civil penalties should be created for inaction by officers, since non-utilization of funds happens mainly because of inaction/discrimination on the part of these officials. Anti-discrimination provisions need to be woven in all schemes and a Grievance-Redressal Cell needs to be created to attend to the complaints of the prospective beneficiaries. Affirmative action policies should be instituted through a system of incentives and disincentives to ensure diversity in our workplaces, in both the private and the public sector. Corporate India must take lead in actualizing this vision.

The Government has made an increase in educational support for the SCs due to increase in educational and livelihood costs, we request that corresponding increase should be made in the educational support for Minorities.

Crisis of Governance: In the years since Independence, the system has miserably failed in delivering development to the

Muslims. But for adequate safeguards and genuine monitoring, the results in future cannot be any different. We need to address this crisis of governance which plagues this nation as a whole and which doubly disadvantages the Muslims. We all need to make the system work through monitoring with penal action against non-performance. Our vision needs to be of accountability to Muslims. It cannot happen if we continue with the purely statistical monitoring as we have seen in the Eleventh Plan. One way of making the system respond is by giving Muslims formal access to the State through empowered Local Entitlement Officers at the Block level, through whom they can exercise some pressure on the system and make it respond. We may also institute formal mechanisms to include Minority group members in monitoring and evaluating the efficacy of schemes and policies directed towards them.

To bring Muslims out of the deep abyss of backwardness in which they continue to sink, new schemes aimed at encouraging civil society groups and NGOs to engage with Muslims need to be structured. Civil society interventions are never a substitute for State action, but they can act as a crucial bridge between Muslims and the State, by initiating pilot schemes and setting realistic benchmarks for successful programming through intensive and closely monitored field level work, by promoting best practices, by refining effective strategies and by undertaking advocacy with the State to make policy changes, which may lead to more effective planning in the future.

Index